THE

Oy of Cooking

A Grandmother's Legacy of Food and Memories

THE

Oy of Cooking

A Grandmother's Legacy of Food and Memories

Susie Weinthal

FOREWORD BY SUZANNE SOMERS

M. Evans and Company, Inc.
New York

First published in Canada by Key Porter Books Limited, 2003

Published in the United States by: M. Evans and Company, Inc., 2005
216 East 49th Street
New York, NY 10017

Library of Congress Cataloging-in-Publication Data

Weinthal, Susie.

The oy of cooking : a grandmother's legacy of food and memories /
[Susie Weinthal].

p. cm.

Includes index.

ISBN 1-59077-094-3

1. Cookery, Jewish.

TX724.W43 2005

641.5'676--dc22

2005021792

Cover design: Peter Maher

Interior design and electronic formatting: Jack Steiner

Printed and bound in the United States of America

9 8 7 6 5 4 3 2 1

Contents

FOR

My children and my grandchildren for inspiring this book

My dear friend Suzanne for telling me to just "do it"

My son Owen for the title

*My editor Andrea Knight for taking me as I am
and pointing me in the right direction*

My designer Jack Steiner for his incredible taste and style

My mentor Malcolm Lester for his hard work, dedication, and integrity

*My publisher Key Porter and senior editor Meg Taylor
for enthusiastically taking a chance on someone new*

And my husband Arthur for loving me so very well

Foreword / **Suzanne Somers**

My friend Susie is the best cook I know. I met her thirty years ago when our now husbands were our boyfriends. We hit it off immediately and have been dearest friends ever since. I liked her style, I liked her wit (she is one of the world's great laughers), I liked her smarts, but most of all, I loved her cooking!

I remember the first thing she made for me on that vacation in Eleuthera where we met. It was her mother's "Choco-Nutto-Grahmo" cookies, just one of what she called her "old neighborhood" recipes from Brooklyn. The cookies were oozing with sweet butter and chocolate, they were crunchy yet smooth, and I spent most of the vacation with my butt sticking out of the refrigerator stealing bite after bite.

Then she made a roast chicken that tasted like no chicken I have ever enjoyed. It was moist and sweet, with a stuffing made from Ritz crackers, sweet peppers, onion, and who knows what else—and I couldn't believe how great it tasted.

Susie and Suzanne.

Thirty years later, having feasted on hundreds, maybe thousands of her meals, I am her greatest fan. Each meal is memorable and each one has me literally licking the plate. Her food is uniquely her own. She can take any recipe and add her own kind of pizzazz, and you find yourself asking for seconds. Her food is not Somersized (following my diet and fitness programs), but where Susie's food is concerned, I make exceptions. One taste and I say to myself, "It's worth it." And it is! You'll love each and every dish.

Learning about food with Susie is like sitting at your mother's knee. Hers is the best kind of food. It's comforting, unbelievably delicious, sexy, mouthwatering, beautiful, and crowd-pleasing. Everybody likes to be invited to one of Susie's famous dinner parties. You know you're going to laugh a lot and you know you're going to have the best meal of the week. Her appetizers, her entrées, and her amazing desserts will wow you.

Try them all—I promise you're gonna love this book!

Introduction

In the beginning ...

I grew up in a frantic Jewish home in Brooklyn where eating was a religion. We ate everything—Italian, Chinese, French, American. And you know that food is really important to me because I am always either eating or planning my next meal. I am a foodie! My DNA is made up of garlic, full-bodied tastes, and the energy to see that it all comes together. My tastes run the gamut from the Jewish food of my heritage, like great chicken soup and matzo balls, to the pork tenderloin I often serve as a "Before" to my guests and the succulent Lobster Fra Diavlo I pour over spaghetti. So, this is not so much a "Jewish" cookbook as a cookbook written by a Jewish grandma.

My creative inner being has tried to come out in many ways in my life. Sometimes, with good results. Every year I begin my spring planting ritual in my vegetable garden—my own patch of land. Seeds and seedlings of leeks, peas, cucumbers, carrots, beets, shallots, and eggplants; the garlic planted last October; radishes and lettuce of all sorts, and, of course, tomatoes. Not a farmer's field, but just enough to feed those I love. For this grandmother, to nurture, feed, water, and create keeps me young and, by summer's end, all these little garden babies of mine will end up on my table. What a trip!

The grandchildren . . . bright, creative, beautiful, feisty, and always hungry. Who better to cook for?

But standing at the kitchen counter washing, chopping, dicing, and, yes, even cursing, is me at my most creative. There is something about cooking that is nourishing and exciting. It requires a good deal of patience and a certain kind of intelligence and courage. It is the most loving gift I have to offer, and so I have spent a great deal of time trying to make the gifts I give memorable.

The recipes in this book are some of my favorites. A hodgepodge assembled over many years. Some from my mother, some from an aunt, some from my children, some from friends, some adapted from other recipes found who knows where, and many of my own invention. They are not complicated, not difficult to make, but all are superb. Great cooking for my family and for my friends.

I didn't express any interest in food until I was able to overcome the traumas that food caused in my childhood. When I was a little girl, food was a source of real trouble for me. I remember when my grandfather gave me an unsolicited puppy. Unsolicited, that is, by my mother. She nearly had a fit when I returned from a Sunday visit at my grandparents with a pup. Naturally, she couldn't simply take it away from me. But when I refused to eat all of my Sunday lunch, she used that as an excuse to deny me my only chance to have a dog of my own.

I was such a bad eater that I was often sent to the bathroom to eat my dinner on top of the laundry hamper. The ultimate degradation! Like many of my generation, I was harangued with stories about "starving children in Europe." How could I be so thoughtless?

So food held little in store for me, other than punishment. But with age came maturity, and I was able to turn to the kitchen. What better place could there be for me? I could work alone—a plus. I could fully explore my senses. I could be active. I could create something. I could nourish those I loved. I could be the matriarch, cooking and feeding. And then, I could fall down exhausted at the dinner table and not be expected to contribute another thing. All this worked in my favor.

We shouldn't forget the genes, though. My own grandmother, Sadie, and my mother, Grandma Jeanne, were both exceptional cooks.

Sadie never used written recipes. She cooked with a handful, a pinch, a bit. I remember well coming downstairs one morning to find her in the kitchen. Callous youth that I was, I said, "Grandma, you won't be here forever, so why don't you give me some of your recipes?"

She began with her incredible rugelach.

"First," she said, "you take a handful of flour."

"Grandma, what is a handful? Is it a cup? A half-cup?"

"A handful!" she said.

"But, Grandma, my hand is much smaller than yours."

With a shrug of her shoulders, she ended any further discussion. And so her great food is lost to us all. This, my friends, is a real tragedy. Trust me.

My mother cooked most meals with her hat on. She'd arrive home from work at 6:00, and by 6:30 we'd sit down to a three-course dinner always served on cloth (table) and with cloth (napkins).

Then Dad would say, "Jeanne, you can take your hat off now."

I determined that my cooking would not be lost to my grandchildren. I started writing down my recipes and recollections for them—Dan, Jessica, Micah, Sarah, Matthew, Adam, and Ruby—to remember me and to remember the women I come from; to one day sit at their own tables, passing on to their families and friends the great food and traditions of welcoming people into their homes.

These recipes are a mixture of all the varieties of food that I have tasted in my life. I never worry about where the ideas come from, just that they taste good. Most of all, the recipes that follow are never difficult to make. Life is too short for fusses and extravaganzas at the table. The recipe directions are in a numbered format—just follow the plan and I know that you will succeed. Enjoy!

Befores and First Courses

When guests arrive for the dinner party, they need drinks and bits to warm them to the group and to satisfy their need to sit right down to eat. Most of the hors d'oeuvres here can be prepared ahead of time so that you're not run ragged at the start of the evening. That will likely come later.

I like to serve at least three hors d'oeuvres, mixing hot and cold, for a dinner party of six to eight people. The seasons obviously dictate my menu. Brie en Croûte is a bit heavy for the summer, but Tomato Bruschetta is really only good then—in the throes of the tomato season.

My husband Arthur, "Pa" to our brood of perfect grandchildren, is of the feeling that once you have had that first glass or two of incredible red wine, what you drink after doesn't hit your palette with the same zing. Great food is like that too. It's the first sip or taste or two that hits your senses. That delights and excites. After that, you numb a bit to the thrill. That's why it's important not to overdo on quantities. Scintillate, but don't satiate. There's more to come.

My friend Suzanne is a woman of substance. Not only does she sing, act, nest well, and write, she is one of the best cooks I know. I always look forward to eating at her home. She will stand in front of her open fridge, staring at the contents until her imagination takes hold and a meal is created. She is not afraid to try anything. A good thing for a cook to do.

I first met Suzanne when she and her husband, Alan, joined Arthur and me in Eleuthera. She was standing outside the local airport holding the rattiest fur coat I'd ever seen. A beautiful, young, voluptuous blond. All that I was not. Alan was inside looking for lost luggage, she said, as she joined us in the car.

"Can I borrow one of your bathing suits? Mine seem to be lost."

Picture this—Suzanne sitting on the beach in my borrowed green bikini, filling it out in all the right places. I never could wear it again.

Suzanne told me then that her ambition in life was to do what Johnny Carson did. I thought DITZ! The girl is mad! How would this sweet innocent ever achieve her goal? Well, the miracle of it is that she did. Laughs on me! Suzanne doesn't pick up on everything she sees and hears—only those things that enhance who she is and what she is. She has always known what she wants.

She'll often say she has learned from me, but, truth be told, I am the student. She has taught me to see the good. To try to turn the other cheek and keep innocence with me whenever I can. I have only ever seen her be soft and gentle, though I know a tiger lurks inside. And most important, she loves her husband as I love mine. The four of us hang together because we have this in common and we live on the same clock. We need to pig out and stretch out at the same time. Dinner dancing is rarely an option. Food and talk are all!

Suzanne's Brie en Croûte

Serves 6 to 8

1½ cups	all-purpose flour	375 mL
8 oz	cream cheese	250 g
½ cup	cold butter	125 mL
2 (5"–6")	Brie cheese rounds	2 (12–15 cm)
Handful	caraway seeds	Handful
1	egg yolk	1

Preheat the oven to 350°F (180°C)

1. **Measure** the flour, cream cheese, and butter into a food processor. Process until just combined, being careful not to overbeat, which will cause the dough to toughen. Place the dough in plastic wrap and refrigerate for 1 hour.

2. **Divide** the dough in half and roll one half into a round shape about 2" (5 cm) larger than the Brie.

If using only one Brie, freeze the remaining dough for up to 6 months.

3. **Sprinkle** the center of each round, an area the size of your Brie, with caraway seeds.

4. **Place** one round of Brie in the center of the dough. Fold flaps over to encase the cheese. With the remaining dough, cut out designs to decorate the top and to ensure that the Brie is properly enclosed.

5. **Brush** lightly beaten egg yolk over the dough. This will help to seal in the cheese and will also help to brown the dough. Bake on a silpat- or parchment-lined baking sheet.

6. **Bake** 40 to 60 minutes or until nicely browned.

7. **Allow** to cool slightly before serving.

I am quite sure in another life I was Italian. There is so much about their food that hits home with me. And I love Italian men. They really look at women.

Mozzarella in Carrozza

Serves 4		
2 cups	olive oil	500 mL
6	anchovy fillets	6
8 slices	white or French bread, 1/4" (5 mm) thick	8 slices
3/4 lb	mozzarella cheese, sliced medium-thin	375 g
2	eggs, lightly beaten with 1/4 tsp (1 mL) kosher or coarse salt	2
1/2 cup	all-purpose flour	125 mL

1. **Melt** the anchovy fillets in $1/4$ cup (50 mL) of heated oil. Set aside.

2. **Cut** the crusts from the bread and cut the slices in half.

3. **Make** a sandwich of bread and mozzarella.

4. **Dip** the sandwich first in the egg and salt and then in the flour. Repeat this process.

5. **Fry** the sandwiches in the remaining hot oil in a large sauté pan until golden brown.

Pour the warm anchovy sauce over the warm bread and serve at once.

My stepson Eric is creative, talented, and sensitive. He has a dream he is chasing. Like all dreamers he has a problem with other people's realities, but like many talented people he might make the dream come true.

The texture of the avocado is crucial to the recipe. If you buy ones that are too ripe, they might be bruised. However, if you buy unripe avocados, they can be hurried along by wrapping them in newspaper and putting them in a drawer for a day or two. I don't know why this works, but it does.

Eric's Guacamole

Serves 8		
4	ripe avocados	4
1/4 cup	finely chopped fresh cilantro leaves,	50 mL
1	garlic clove, chopped very fine	1
	kosher or coarse salt to taste	
1	lime, juiced	1
1	good-sized fresh tomato, diced to 1/2" (1 cm)	1
1/2	white onion (not Spanish, and not the usual yellow) diced to 1/2" (1 cm)	1/2
2	canned chipotles, diced	2
	Adobo sauce to taste	
1/4 cup	fresh cilantro leaves, for garnish	50 mL

1. **Mash** the avocados with the chopped cilantro, garlic, and salt in a big non-metal mixing bowl.

2. **Stir** in the lime juice, most of the tomato and onion, and the chipotles.

3. **Stir** in the adobo sauce that comes with the chipotles and taste as you go. Check for heat comfort and add more adobo sauce if desired. Mix well.

4. **Put** into a serving dish, ideally a color that contrasts (but works with) the green.

5. **Scatter** the rest of the diced tomato, onion, and cilantro leaves on top.

Serve with yellow or blue tortilla chips and tequila.

These are delicious and best of all they can be prepared well in advance. I overmake the croustades so that I generally have some in the freezer. Just in case.

Mushroom Croustades

Serves 6 to 8

Croustades:

2 Tbsp	soft butter	25 mL
36 slices	fresh white bread	36 slices

Mushroom duxelles filling:

4 Tbsp	finely chopped shallots	50 mL
¾ lb	mushrooms, finely chopped	375 g
4 Tbsp	butter	50 mL
2 Tbsp	all-purpose flour	25 mL
1 cup	heavy cream	250 mL
½ tsp	kosher or coarse salt	2 mL
¼ tsp	cayenne	1 mL
3 Tbsp	finely chopped Italian parsley	45 mL
2 Tbsp	finely chopped chives	25 mL
½ tsp	fresh lemon juice	2 mL
2 Tbsp	grated Parmigiano-Reggiano cheese	25 mL
	Butter	

Preheat the oven to 400°F (200°C)

For the croustades:

1. **Coat** the inside of 1" (5 cm) muffin tins with the butter, using a pastry brush or paper towel.

2. **Cut** a round from each slice of bread with a 2" (8 cm) cutter or glass. Save the scraps to make fresh bread crumbs for other uses.

3. **Carefully fit** the rounds into the muffin tins, pushing the center of the bread into the well and gently pressing it around the bottom of the tin with the tip of your finger. Be careful not to tear the bread, as each round should form a perfect little cup that won't leak.

4. **Bake** the croustades for about 10 minutes, or until they brown lightly on the rims. Remove the croustades and let cool.

The unfilled croustades freeze well. Without defrosting them, fill with the creamed duxelles and heat as described. I often double the recipe for the croustades, freeze them, and then make a fresh batch of duxelles as required.

For the duxelles:

5. **Chop** the shallots and then the mushrooms very, very fine.

6. **Melt** the butter slowly in a 12″ (30 cm) frying pan and add the shallots. Stir for about 2 to 3 minutes without letting them brown.

7. **Stir** in the mushrooms. Mix them well into the butter and see that they are thoroughly coated before leaving them on their own. In a few minutes, they will begin to give off a good deal of moisture. Stir them from time to time, and continue to cook until all the moisture has evaporated, 10 to 15 minutes. Don't add any salt as it will cause the mushrooms to sweat.

8. **Remove** the pan from the heat.

9. **Sprinkle** the flour over the mushrooms and stir thoroughly together until not a trace is visible.

10. **Pour** the cream over this mixture and, stirring continuously, bring it to a boil over medium heat. It will thicken heavily.

11. **Turn down** the heat to the barest simmer and cook a minute or two longer to remove the taste of flour.

12. **Remove** the pan from the heat and stir in the salt, cayenne, parsley, chives, and lemon juice.

13. **Taste** for seasoning and transfer the duxelles to a bowl to cool; then cover with plastic wrap and refrigerate until ready for use.

The duxelles can be prepared one day in advance.

Preheat the oven to 350°F (180°C)

14. **Fill** the croustades, using a small spoon. Sprinkle each one with a bit of cheese, dot with a speck of butter, and arrange on a lined cookie sheet.

15. **Heat** the filled croustades for 10 minutes in the oven, then briefly under the broiler, but watch carefully, as they burn easily.

Serve warm just out of the oven. Delicious!

This bruschetta recipe is easy and delicious. The tomatoes can be prepared the morning of the day required, so the only last-minute task is toasting the bread. Like many of my tomato recipes, I only make this dish at the height of tomato season.

Bruschetta con Pomodoro

Serves 4

2	beefsteak tomatoes	2
½ tsp	balsamic vinegar	2 mL
¼ tsp	granulated sugar	1 mL
½	garlic clove, minced	½
	Kosher or coarse salt and freshly ground pepper to taste	
8 slices	Italian bread, ½" (1 cm) thick	8 slices
1	garlic clove, halved	1
4 Tbsp	olive oil	50 mL

Preheat the oven to 500°F (260°C)

1. **Peel,** seed, and chop the tomatoes into $1/4"$ (5 mm) pieces. (See "Susie's Rules," page 267, for tips on peeling tomatoes.)

2. **Combine** in a small bowl the tomatoes, balsamic vinegar, sugar, minced garlic, salt, and pepper to taste. Marinate for at least 2 hours.

3. **Toast** the bread slices on a baking sheet in the upper third of the preheated oven for 5 minutes, or until they are golden. While the toasts are warm, rub them with the garlic and brush both sides with oil.

4. **Top** the toasts with the tomato mixture and serve warm.

My sister-in-law, Halina, gave this recipe to me. Really tasty and best of all, you can make it far in advance, freeze it, and then just heat it up. The recipe must be very old because when I was going through my mother's recipes, I found it there, too.

Spinach Balls

Serves 8

¼ cup	butter or margarine	50 mL
2	onions, finely chopped	2
2	garlic cloves, minced	2
2	boxes (each 10 oz/ 283 g) frozen spinach, chopped	2
2 cups	herb bread stuffing mix, or homemade seasoned bread crumbs (see page 247)	500 mL
½ cup	butter or margarine, melted	125 mL
6	eggs, beaten	6
½ cup	grated Parmigiano-Reggiano cheese	125 mL
1½ tsp	dried thyme	7 mL

Preheat the oven to 350°F (180°C)

1. **Heat** the ¼ cup (50 mL) of butter or margarine and sauté the onion and garlic until soft. Set aside.
2. **Cook** the spinach according to the directions on the package, drain it, and squeeze it dry.
3. **Mix** all the remaining ingredients together.
4. **Chill** for 2 hours.
5. **Form** the spinach mixture into balls using about 1 tablespoon (15 mL) of the mixture.
6. **Bake** for 20 minutes on a silpat- or parchment-lined baking sheet and serve warm.

The spinach balls can be frozen and reheated just before serving.

I could make a meal out of these wings and sometimes do. I must admit that I am not always a gracious hostess, grabbing my good food right alongside my guests. Apart from being delicious, much of this recipe can be prepared in advance.

Crispy Chicken Wings with Blue Cheese Dip

Serves 8

Wings:

3 lbs	chicken wings (about 32)	1.5 kg
1/4 tsp	cayenne	1 mL
1 tsp	dry mustard powder	5 mL
1 1/2 tsp	cumin	7 mL
1 tsp	paprika	5 mL
1/2 tsp	kosher or coarse salt	2 mL
1/4 tsp	freshly ground black pepper	1 mL

Dip:

2 oz	blue cheese, crumbled	50 g
1/4 cup	mayonnaise	50 mL
1/4 cup	sour cream	50 mL
1 tsp	Tabasco sauce	5 mL
1 tsp	dried tarragon	5 mL
1/4 tsp	kosher or coarse salt	1 mL
	Freshly ground pepper to taste	

Preheat the oven to 425°F (220°C)

1. **Wash** the wings well, remove any feathers, and cut into three pieces. Freeze the wing tips for making stock. Pat the other pieces dry and set aside.

2. **Combine** the cayenne, dry mustard, cumin, paprika, salt, and pepper (this can be done a day in advance).

3. **Arrange** the wings in single layer on a rack set over a cookie sheet. Rub each wing with the spices. You can refrigerate the wings at this stage on their tray, covered with plastic wrap. Save any leftover spice to sprinkle over the wings just before baking.

4. **Bake** in a preheated oven, turning them once, for 20 minutes per side or until very crisp.

For the dip:

5. **Combine** the ingredients for the dip in a food processor or blender. The dip can be prepared a day in advance.

Serve the wings hot out of the oven with the dip.

Grandma Jeanne's Shrimp Toast

Serves 4

½ lb	raw shrimp	250 g
	Juice of 1 lemon	
1	small onion, grated	1
1 Tbsp	cornstarch	15 mL
1 tsp	kosher or coarse salt	5 mL
1 tsp	granulated sugar	5 mL
2	eggs, beaten	2
1	can (7 oz/200 mL) water chestnuts, drained and diced	1
8 slices	white sandwich bread, with crusts removed	8 slices
¾ cup	vegetable shortening	175 mL

1. **Clean** the shrimp and cut coarsely. (See "Susie's Rules," page 267, for cleaning shrimp.)

2. **Sprinkle** the shrimp with the lemon juice.

3. **Mix** the onion with the cornstarch, salt, and sugar in a large bowl.

4. **Stir** in the beaten eggs, water chestnuts, and shrimp.

5. **Cut** the bread slices into quarters on the diagonal. You will have 32 slices.

6. **Spread** about 1 teaspoon (5 mL) of the mixture on one side of each triangle. Cover the surface of the bread completely.

7. **Melt** the vegetable shortening in a hot sauté pan until the temperature reaches 350°F (180°C) on a candy thermometer.

8. **Deep-fry** the bread, shrimp side down. When the bottoms are browned, about 1 minute, carefully turn and cook on the reverse side till browned.

9. **Drain** on paper towel.

Serve immediately.

I am almost, but not quite, embarrassed to give you a recipe for such a dish. Dated and commonplace, but frankly delicious. When my stomach starts to bulge too much and I know I must resist any "carb" treats, this is what I stuff my mouth with.

Shrimp Cocktail

Serves 4		
1 lb	raw shrimp	500 g
4 cups	water	1 L
1	celery stalk, sliced	1
1	small onion, sliced	1
1	carrot, sliced	1
	Juice of 1 lemon	
1 tsp	kosher or coarse salt	5 mL
½ tsp	freshly ground pepper	2 mL

Sauce:

½ cup	hot white horseradish	125 mL
½ cup	red chili sauce	125 mL
3 or 4 drops	Tabasco sauce, to taste	3 or 4 drops

1. **Gently pull** the shells off the shrimp, leaving the tails attached. Clean the shrimp. (See "Susie's Rules," page 267, for cleaning shrimp.) DO NOT throw away the shells, but rather add them to the stock.

2. **Bring** the water to a boil in a large saucepan. Add all the ingredients, including the shells but not the shrimp. Boil for 10 minutes.

3. **Add** the shrimp and simmer, uncovered, until they turn pink. Depending on the size of the shrimp, this should take about 3 or 4 minutes.

4. **Remove** the shrimp from the broth and store in a plastic bag, placing it over a bowl of ice to cool.

For the sauce:

5. **Mix** the horseradish, chili sauce, and Tabasco together. When serving, squeeze some fresh lemon over the cooled shrimp and serve with the sauce on the side.

Great-Grandma Sadie Freifeld was the cook in the family. Like so many women of her generation, cooking was her life. My mom, Grandma Jeanne, had all of her talents but none of her patience.

My mother, "Grandma Jeanne," 1929.

When my mother retired, she turned her incredible energy to cooking. She'd read and collect recipes and became quite adventurous in the kitchen. Her home was open to all friends and family. She was a wonderful hostess. The house was cleaned, there were flowers (a new concept to her generation), and lots and lots of food. Her motto was never to worry about leftovers. Just make sure that there is enough for the family and anyone else who happens by.

My mother had a date every Saturday night with the "girls" and their husbands. The "girls" were not girls at all. They were her group of friends—foxy ladies, like my mother, with incredible killer instincts. These women were all first-generation. Talk about upwardly mobile. From poor beginnings, these friends of my mother had moved to Brooklyn, bought their own homes, and started their families. Their husbands were uneducated but smart. They worked hard, didn't drink, didn't carouse, and came home to the family every night for 6:30 dinner.

The "girls" did not work. They shopped, played cards, went to the hairdressers, cooked, and entertained amongst themselves. That is, all but my mother. She alone was a businesswoman. When the Depression came, she had to work to help my father. After that, the need was all hers. She wanted beautiful things and worked to get them.

She was a dynamo, with energy to work, shop, flirt, and play mah jong and cards, all the while running a strict household that shook at her every command. Her drive was sublime.

She left us kids (my brother, Larry, and me) to the care of "the help" as she went out into the business world as a bookkeeper. She was one of the first who made her way as a freelancer. A true independent. The people she worked for loved her. The men often stopped by the house to pick her up to take her to work. They loved her because she was competent, capable, charming, and gracious.

When working in the garment district, she once baked a cake for a well-known dress designer who had refused her entry into his showroom. Wouldn't let her get it wholesale. The cake changed that.

Her most remarkable quality was her ability to be competent, assertive, and tough, while at the same time maintaining her delicious femininity and sexuality. But what a mother. Demanding, demanding, demanding, and then demanding more. Top this off with her father's dreadful temper. She was not easy. The house was filled with her anger, also from her father, giving me a stomach ache. Having ceded control to his wife, whom he believed knew what was best, my father would sit and read, ignoring all. My brother fought her all the time, adding to the stomach ache.

I was a good girl because she terrified me. But I knew all the time she loved me to pieces. She'd hug and kiss me and would look at me, most of the time, with love in her eyes. In spite of all of that love, she could destroy. Her term of endearment for me was *measkite* (the Yiddish word for funny-looking). When I was sixteen, she was shocked to find that I thought I was ugly. How on earth could I be so "stupid"—one of her favorite descriptions.

"If I really thought you were funny-looking, do you think I would have called you *measkite*?"

"Try to explain that to a four-year-old, Mom," I said.

And I was the stupid one?

Even though she took, my mother gave in spades. She gave me her business acumen, her competence, her love of home and family, her taste—oh! and her love of spending—and, most important, she taught me that I could be whatever I wanted. She never told me that I couldn't do something just because I was a girl. That was a great gift.

There is rarely a Jewish holiday that goes by without gefilte fish as an appetizer. However, my mom would often slice it in bite-size pieces with red horseradish on the side and serve with a cocktail. My favorite brand of prepared gefilte fish is Old Vienna.

Grandma Jeanne's Quick Gefilte Fish

Serves 8		
16 pieces	prepared gefilte fish	**16 pieces**
2	onions, quartered	2
3	celery stalks with their leaves	3
3	carrots, sliced	3
	Bouquet garni (see "Susie's Rules," page 262)	

1. **Drain** the fish and reserve.

2. **Add** the remaining ingredients to the liquid (gel) in a large saucepan with enough water to double the volume.

3. **Bring** to boil, and then simmer slowly for 15 minutes, being careful that the stock does not boil down.

4. **Add** the fish pieces and cook slowly for an additional 15 minutes.

5. **Gently** remove the fish and carrots to a covered container. Strain the liquid over the fish and refrigerate.

Serve cold with spicy hot horseradish.

Grandma Jeanne's Salmon Mousse

Serves 8

Mousse:

1	envelope (1 Tbsp/15 mL) unflavored gelatin	1
½ cup	sour cream	125 mL
½ cup	mayonnaise	125 mL
2 Tbsp	fresh lemon juice	25 mL
1	large onion, chopped	1
½ tsp	Tabasco sauce	2 mL
¼ tsp	paprika	1 mL
1 tsp	kosher or coarse salt	5 mL
1	can (1 lb/500 g) salmon	1
1 cup	heavy (35%) cream	250 mL

Dressing:

½ cup	sour cream	125 mL
1 cup	sliced and seeded cucumber	250 mL
¼ cup	finely chopped fresh dill	50 mL
¼ cup	thinly sliced green onions	50 mL

For the mousse:

1. **Soften** the gelatin in $^{1}/_{4}$ cup (50 mL) cold water, add $^{1}/_{2}$ cup (125 mL) boiling water, and cool.

2. **Mix** together the sour cream, mayonnaise, lemon juice, onion, Tabasco, paprika, and salt.

3. **Remove** the bones and juice of the salmon, add the salmon to the mousse mixture, and combine well.

4. **Add** the gelatin mixture and combine.

5. **Whip** the cream and then fold into the mixture. Chill.

For the dressing:

6. **Mix** together the sour cream, cucumbers, dill, and green onions.

Serve with the mousse and some crunchy crackers.

I always have some gravlax in my freezer. The fish is good, but the sauce is great. Can't have one without the other.

Gravlax and Dill Sauce

Each ½ lb (250 g) serves 8

3 bunches	fresh dill	3 bunches
½ cup	granulated sugar	125 mL
2 Tbsp	crushed white peppercorns	25 mL
	Juice of 2 lemons	
¼ cup (heaping)	kosher or coarse salt	60 mL
2	salmon fillets, each 2 lbs (1 kg), with skin on	2

Dill sauce for each ½ lb serving:

2 Tbsp	honey mustard	25 mL
1 Tbsp	Dijon mustard	15 mL
1 Tbsp	granulated sugar	15 mL
	Kosher or coarse salt and freshly ground pepper to taste	
1 Tbsp	white vinegar	15 mL
⅓ cup	vegetable oil	75 mL
½ cup	finely chopped fresh dill	125 mL

1. **Spread** half of the dill on the bottom of a 9″ × 13″ (24 cm × 33 cm) pan. Mix sugar, peppercorns, lemon juice, and salt together and rub into the salmon.

2. **Place** one piece of salmon on top of the dill in the pan and spread the remaining dill over the salmon. Place the second piece on top of the first piece.

3. **Cover** the salmon well with plastic wrap or foil. Then place bricks or very heavy cans on top of the covered salmon.

4. **Refrigerate** and turn the salmon every 12 hours for 3 days.

5. **Remove** the dill and peppercorns and cut the salmon into eight pieces. Wrap well and freeze for up to 6 months.

To serve, slice very thin when the salmon is still slightly frozen.

For the dill dipping sauce:

You can use the blender or food processor for this step.

6. **Whisk** together the mustards, sugar, salt, pepper and vinegar.

7. **Slowly add** the oil while whisking, until the sauce is smooth and thick. Fold in the dill.

The sauce can be prepared a day in advance. Refrigerate until serving.

When I was a girl growing up in Brooklyn, this is what you ate. Lots of meat, potato—starch was required—and a green vegetable that was cooked till it screamed. Liver was healthy, kishka was good, and butter was fine. Three glasses of milk a day. I wonder what the conventional wisdom will be 10 years from now. Could lettuce be bad?

Note carefully, this recipe is for "mock" kishka. Not the real thing. No butter. Margarine!

Grandma Jeanne's Mock Kishka

Serves 8		
2	medium carrots	2
2	celery stalks	2
2 or 3	onions	2 or 3
1	box (8 oz/250 g) Tam Tam crackers (Manischewitz egg matzo crackers)	1
	Kosher or coarse salt and freshly ground pepper to taste	
½ cup	margarine, melted	125 g
	Vegetable spray	

Preheat the oven to 350°F (180°C)

1. **Place** the carrots, celery, onions, and Tam Tam crackers in a food processor and process until a medium chop is obtained.

2. **Put** in a large bowl and add the salt and pepper and the melted margarine. Blend well.

3. **Lightly spray** three 12" (30 cm) pieces of aluminum foil with vegetable spray. Divide the mixture into three parts.

4. **Roll** each section of the kishka in the three pieces of foil, like a thick banana, twisting the ends to close.

5. **Bake** for 1 hour. Remove the foil and cool the kishka.

6. **Slice** into pieces about ½" (1 cm) thick.

You can serve the kishka warm or you can rewrap it in foil and freeze. Heat the frozen kishka at 350°F (180°C) for 30 minutes, until hot through.

Grandma Jeanne's Meatballs

Serves 8

Meatballs:

3 lbs	ground beef (chuck and neck)	1.5 kg
1	large onion, grated	1
Scant cup	bread crumbs (see page 247)	225 mL
2 Tbsp	ketchup	25 mL
1/2 cup	tomato paste	50 mL
	Kosher or coarse salt and freshly ground pepper to taste	
1 cup	water	250 mL
1 Tbsp	vegetable oil	15 mL

Sauce:

1 cup	fresh lemon juice	250 mL
1 cup	brown sugar	250 mL
5 cups	chicken broth, homemade preferred	1.25 L
1/2 cup	tomato paste	125 mL
3	whole gingersnaps	3

For the meatballs:

1. **Mix** (I use my clean hands) to combine the meat, onions, bread crumbs, ketchup, tomato paste, salt, pepper, and water.

2. **Shape** into 1" (2.5 cm) meatballs.

3. **Heat** the vegetable oil in a hot sauté pan till quite hot and brown the meatballs in batches.

For the sauce:

4. **Mix** together the sauce ingredients and add to the meatballs.

5. **Simmer** uncovered for 45 minutes. Add the gingersnaps to thicken the gravy.

Serve warm.

This is a favorite of mine because I can prepare it well in advance. Make sure that you warn your guests about the hot mustard. I slice the cooled tenderloin and place it on a platter with one bowl of plum sauce and one of hot mustard.

Pork Tenderloin

Serves 8		
1½ Tbsp	soy sauce	20 mL
1	garlic clove, minced	1
2½ Tbsp	hoisin sauce	30 mL
2 lbs	fresh pork tenderloin	1 kg
½ cup	plum sauce	125 mL
¼ cup	powdered hot mustard	50 mL

1. **Mix** the soy sauce, garlic, and hoisin sauce together and rub on the pork tenderloin.

2. **Set aside** for at least 1 hour to marinate.

Preheat the oven to 300°F (150°C)

3. **Put** the pork tenderloin pieces on a rack over 2 cups (500 mL) of water in a roasting pan. Do not let the meat touch the water, and add more hot water if necessary to keep the bottom of the pan covered with water during cooking. This serves to steam the pork.

4. After 45 minutes, **brush** the meat with the sauce. Turn it over, brushing the other side with the remaining mixture.

5. **Cook** for another 30 minutes.

6. **Slice** thinly and serve hot with plum sauce or Chinese mustard.

To make the Chinese mustard: Dilute powdered mustard with cold water until you reach the consistency of regular mustard.

Soups

I make all my soups well in advance of any dinner party. When they cool a bit, I transfer the soup to a zip-lock plastic bag and mark the contents and date on the bag. Remove any air in the bag before closing and then lay it flat on a cookie sheet in the freezer until ready for use. Once the soup is frozen, remove the cookie sheet and stack the soups in the freezer. You can store a lot of soup this way and never, ever get freezer burn.

Then there's the eating. Soup is a very filling first course and I don't overdo on the size of the portions. I've recently switched from serving it in large bowls to smaller ones. Just a taste or two is enough for a dinner party. Remember that there's a lot more to come.

Not only is my husband the brightest, sexiest, funniest, and most interesting man I know, he makes great soup! What more could a woman want?

Pa's Bean, Barley, and Mushroom Soup

Serves 10 to 12

6 strips	beef flanken with bones, cut into pieces (best purchased from a kosher butcher)	6 strips
3–4	beef (sugar) bones (The butcher should give these to you as a gift—especially if you smile sweetly.)	3–4
1 cup	pearl barley, washed with cold water	250 mL
¾ cup	dried mushrooms	175 mL
1 cup	white lima beans, washed with cold water	250 mL
4	onions, diced	4
1	carrot, cut into bite-size pieces	1
1 bunch	dill, finely chopped	1 bunch
5	celery stalks with their greens, diced	5
2	large parsnips, whole	2
2 Tbsp	kosher or coarse salt	25 mL
1 tsp	freshly ground pepper	5 mL

1. **Place** the meat and soup bones in a large pot and cover with water.
2. **Add** the pearl barley. Bring to a boil. Reduce the heat to low and simmer for 1 hour. Skim the foam as it rises to the top.
3. **Cool** in the pot in the refrigerator overnight.
4. **Cover** the dried mushrooms in hot water and soak for 30 minutes. Lift the mushrooms from the liquid, squeezing them over the bowl to remove as much moisture as possible. Rinse the mushrooms very lightly to remove any dirt.
5. **Chop** the mushrooms finely.
6. **Strain** the soaking liquid through a sieve lined with a damp cheesecloth and set aside.
7. **Remove** the fat from the top of the cooled soup.
8. **Add** the lima beans, onions, carrot, dill, celery, and parsnip to the soup.
9. **Stir** in the mushrooms and the strained mushroom liquid.
10. **Bring** to a boil, then reduce to a simmer. Cook, covered, for 1 hour.
11. **Discard** the sugar bones.
12. **Season** with salt and pepper to taste.

The soup can be frozen. It is best prepared a day or two in advance.

Like most things we cook, tasting, tasting, and tasting is crucial. You might want to adjust the sugar or the lemon juice in this recipe till you get it just right. Be my guest.

Cabbage Soup

Serves 8		
2 lbs	short ribs or strips of flanken (best purchased at a kosher butcher shop)	1 kg
2	beef (sugar) bones	2
2	onions, diced	2
1	can (28 oz/796 mL) Italian plum tomatoes	1
1	cabbage, preferably Savoy, thinly sliced	1
1 Tbsp	kosher or coarse salt	15 mL
½ tsp	freshly ground pepper	2 mL
	Juice of 2 lemons	
½–¾ cup	brown sugar	125–175 mL
3 Tbsp	tomato paste	45 mL

1. **Put** the meat and bones into a stockpot with enough cold water to cover, plus 1" (2.5 cm). Bring to a boil and skim off the foam that will rise to the top.

2. **Add** the onions and tomatoes, squeezing them with your hand as you put them into the pot to break them up. Be careful—they tend to spit.

3. **Cover** and cook over low heat for 1 hour.

4. **Stir** in the cabbage, salt, and pepper and cover and cook for 1 hour.

5. **Stir** in the lemon juice, brown sugar, and tomato paste.

6. **Cook** for about 20 minutes and taste for seasoning.

Mushroom Soup

Serves 8

1 oz	dried porcini mushrooms	25 g
1 cup	hot chicken stock	250 mL
1	leek, white part only	1
10 Tbsp	butter	150 mL
1 cup	diced shallots	250 mL
1 cup	diced onion	250 mL
3	garlic cloves, minced	3
3 cups	finely chopped celery	750 mL
1 lb	fresh shiitake mushrooms sliced and stemmed (dispose of the stems)	500 g
1 lb	fresh crimini mushrooms, sliced and stemmed	500 g
1 lb	fresh oyster mushrooms, sliced and stemmed	500 g
½ cup	white wine	125 mL
½ cup	dry sherry	125 mL
4 Tbsp	all-purpose flour	50 mL
8 cups	chicken stock, homemade preferred	2 L
	Kosher or coarse salt and freshly ground pepper to taste	
¼ tsp	cayenne pepper	1 mL
2 cups	heavy (35%) cream	500 mL
6 Tbsp	Italian parsley, chopped	90 mL

1. **Put** the dried porcini in a bowl, add the 1 cup (250 mL) of hot stock and let stand about 30 minutes. Lift out the porcini, squeezing them over the bowl to remove as much moisture as possible. Rinse to remove any remaining grit. Chop the mushrooms finely. Strain the soaking liquid through a sieve lined with damp cheesecloth and set aside.

2. **Clean** and finely chop the leeks. (See "Susie's Rules," page 265, for cleaning leeks)

3. **Melt** 4 tablespoons (50 mL) of the butter over medium-high heat in a stockpot. Add the leek, shallots, onion, garlic, and celery and sauté until the onion is translucent, about 10 minutes.

4. **Stir** in 4 tablespoons (50 mL) of butter and the fresh mushrooms, stirring until they give off their juices and soften, 10 to 15 minutes.

5. **Add** the chopped porcini and their strained mushroom liquid and heat through.

6. **Stir** in the white wine and the sherry. Boil until the liquid is reduced.

7. **Melt** the remaining 2 tablespoons (25 mL) of the butter in a medium saucepan. Sprinkle in the flour, stirring constantly until all traces of flour disappear, about 2 minutes.

8. **Remove** from the heat, pour in 1 cup (250 mL) of the stock, and whisk to blend smoothly. Pour in the remaining chicken stock and bring to a boil, stirring continuously to ensure you don't scorch the soup. The soup base will be slightly thickened and should coat the bottom of a spoon lightly.

9. **Season** with salt and pepper.

10. **Add** the soup base to the mushrooms. Reduce the heat to low and simmer, uncovered, for about 20 minutes.

11. **Purée** the mixture in a blender until smooth.

12. **Season** again with salt and pepper and a bit of cayenne pepper to taste.

13. **Stir** in the cream.

Serve warm and sprinkle with the chopped parsley.

A wonderful soup for entertaining. The Stilton wontons give the soup a lift of taste and crunch.

Jane's Broccoli Soup with Wontons

Serves 8

Soup:

1	leek	1
3 Tbsp	unsalted butter	45 mL
1	onion, chopped	1
3	garlic cloves, chopped	3
3 lbs	broccoli (about 2 large heads)	1.5 kg
4 cups	chicken stock, homemade preferred	1 L
½ cup	heavy (35%) cream	125 mL
	Kosher or coarse salt and freshly ground pepper to taste	

Stilton wontons:

5 oz	Stilton cheese	140 g
¼ cup	chopped fresh chives	50 mL
8	wonton wrappers	8
1	egg, beaten, for glaze	
	Vegetable oil (for deep frying)	

For the soup:

1. **Clean** and chop the leeks. (See "Susie's Rules," page 265, for cleaning leeks.)

2. **Melt** the butter in a large stockpot over medium heat. Add the leek, onion, and garlic. Sauté for about 10 minutes, or until lightly browned.

3. **Coarsely chop** the broccoli florets. Peel the stem and chop.

4. **Sauté** the broccoli pieces for 5 minutes.

5. **Add** the stock and bring to a boil. Reduce the heat and simmer until the broccoli is tender, about 20 minutes.

6. **Purée** the mixture in batches in a blender and then return to the stockpot.

7. **Stir** in the cream and simmer for 10 minutes.

8. **Season** with salt and pepper.

The soup can be prepared a day ahead. Cover tightly and refrigerate.

For the Stilton wontons:

9. **Mix** the Stilton and chives in small bowl.

10. **Place** 2 teaspoons (10 mL) of the cheese mixture in the center of each wonton.

11. **Brush** the glaze around the wonton edges. This will help keep them closed while cooking. Fold the wontons in half, forming triangles. Using your fingertips, firmly press the edges to seal.

12. When ready to serve, **heat** the vegetable oil in a deep fryer or large heavy saucepan.

13. **Carefully lower** the wontons into the oil and cook until golden brown, about 1 minute, turning occasionally.

14. Using a slotted spoon, **transfer** the wontons to paper towels and drain.

15. **Bring** the soup to a simmer. Ladle into bowls. Top each serving with two hot wontons.

As part of their assimilation into American ways, my parents gradually gave up most of the Jewish practices that they had been brought up with. They no longer kept a kosher home and rarely went to synagogue, but considered themselves Jews without any question. I was sent to Hebrew School, and my brother, Larry, celebrated his bar mitzvah. Ethically, morally, and traditionally, we were Jews.

Rosh Hashanah and Yom Kippur were sacrosanct. There was to be no kidding around. While our home was run, over-run, governed, and ruled by my mother, on the three days encompassed by these two holidays, the roles were reversed. Only on these three days. Both parents came home from work quite early. My mom had prepared a traditional supper and we ate in the dining room. Somehow it was never quite right enough for my

My parents in 1926, just after they were married.

father. He was rushed and irritable, bickering with my mother over the timing of the meal and whatever else he could find fault with. It was really quite shocking. Only on these three days. I've never understood why, but mother never argued back and took whatever he gave.

My father was a distant man. He loved my mother to distraction and above all else, including me. Six months before he died at the age of eighty-eight he finally told me that he loved me. At least I did get to hear it, but the mark had already been left. Men of that generation weren't particularly involved with their children, particularly girls, and they withheld their affection. While my mother was frightening, my dad was thoroughly intimidating. Cold!

On these holidays, however, I was allowed to go to synagogue, where my dad had been all day, to pick him up. I would sneak in and find him in the sanctuary. Time after time, we would sit together in those last moments of the day, when he would have me listen to the beauty of the choir. It was always the music that got to him. Then we would walk home silently, but together. Only on these three days.

No Jewish holiday would be complete without chicken soup. It would be like a hot dog without mustard, a martini without an olive, chocolate cake without cold milk.

I buy enough chicken to make the soup, then chicken in the pot, and then chicken salad. We prefer dark meat, so I buy four legs and thighs. However, if you are a white meat eater, buy the whole chicken. I wrap the chicken in cheesecloth for easy removal from the pot.

After the cooked soup chills, remove the layer of fat at the top of the bowl. If you are not using the soup immediately, pour the stock into eight or more ice cube trays. When the stock is frozen, empty the cubes into a freezer bag and keep them for up to 3 months. Great when you just need a bit of stock.

Chicken Soup

Serves 10

1	whole chicken, or 4 chicken legs and thighs and 2 lbs (1 kg) chicken bones and wings	1
1	large white onion, with the skin on, quartered	1
4	medium carrots, scrubbed and cut into 1" (2.5 cm) chunks	4
2	medium parsnips, scrubbed and cut into 1" (2.5 cm) chunks	2
2	leeks	2
2	large shallots	2
3	celery stalks with their greens	3
	Bouquet garni (see "Susie's Rules,"page 262)	
1	garlic clove	1
	Kosher or coarse salt, to taste	
½ **tsp**	white pepper	2 mL

1. **Place** the washed chicken and the bones in a stock-pot with enough cold water to cover, plus 2" (5 cm).

2. **Bring to** a boil over high heat, skimming the foam as it rises to the top until the broth is clear.

3. **Clean** and slice the leeks. (See "Susie's Rules," page 265, for cleaning leeks.)

4. **Add** the onion, carrots, parsnips, leeks, shallots, celery, bouquet garni, and garlic.

5. **Season** with salt and pepper.

6. **Reduce** the heat to low and simmer until the vegetables are tender and the meat begins to fall off the bones, about 3 hours.

7. **Check** your seasoning.

8. **Before** you strain the soup, remember to leave the dregs (the bits of pepper and small bones) behind.

9. **Remove** the chicken and the vegetables from the soup and reserve.

10. **Pass** the liquid through a fine sieve lined with wet cheesecloth into a large container and refrigerate overnight so the fat rises to the top and hardens.

11. **Carefully remove** any fat from the surface and discard.

Nothing is more delicious than a supper of boiled chicken just out of the pot.

See page 21 for storing soup.

Matzo Balls

Makes 24

1 cup	matzo meal	250 mL
¼ cup	corn oil or melted chicken fat (I prefer the fat— see "Susie's Rules," page 264)	125 mL
1 cup	hot water	250 mL
3	large eggs	3
½ tsp	kosher or coarse salt	2 mL
¼ tsp	freshly ground pepper	1 mL

1. **Stir** the matzo meal and the melted fat into 1 cup of hot water.

2. **Mix** in the eggs and seasoning to the mixture.

3. **Cover** and refrigerate overnight or for a minimum of 1 to 2 hours.

4. **Line** a baking pan with parchment paper.

5. **Bring** a large pot of water to a boil.

6. **Dampen** your fingertips, and form 2 heaping tablespoons (25 mL) of the batter into a 1 ½" (4 cm) ball, being careful not to compress the mixture too much, and place the ball on the pan.

7. **Form** the remaining balls.

8. **Gently slide** the matzo balls into the boiling water. Reduce the heat to medium. Cover and cook for 45 minutes.

9. **To test** for doneness, remove a ball from the water and slice it in half. The color should be light throughout.

Matzo balls can be stored in the cooked chicken soup.

French Onion Soup

Serves 2

3 Tbsp	unsalted butter	45 mL
1 Tbsp	olive oil	15 mL
2 lbs	white onions, sliced thinly	1 kg
Pinch	granulated sugar	Pinch
	Kosher or coarse salt and freshly ground pepper	
2 Tbsp	all-purpose flour	25 mL
4 cups	beef broth	1 L
½ cup	white wine	125 mL
	Bouquet garni (see "Susie's Rules," page 262)	
3 Tbsp	cognac	45 mL
8 slices	crusty French bread, ½" (1 cm) thick	8 slices
1 Tbsp	butter, melted	15 mL
1	large garlic clove, halved	1
1½ cups	freshly grated Gruyère cheese	375 mL
⅓ cup	freshly grated Parmigiano-Reggiano cheese	75 mL

1. **Melt** the butter with the oil in a large, heated saucepan. Add the onions.

2. **Add** the sugar, salt, and pepper to taste and cook over moderately low heat, covered, stirring occasionally, until the onions are soft, about 10 minutes.

3. **Uncover** and cook over moderate heat, stirring occasionally, until golden brown, about 20 minutes.

4. **Add** the flour and cook, stirring, for 2 minutes.

5. **Add** the broth, wine, bouquet garni, and more salt and pepper to taste, and cook, partially covered, skimming occasionally, for 30 minutes.

6. **Add** the cognac.

Preheat the oven to 350°F (180°C)

7. **Arrange** the sliced bread on a baking sheet, brush both sides with melted butter, and bake, turning once, for 10 minutes, or until golden. Rub the toasts with garlic while they are still warm.

8. **Transfer** the soup to ovenproof bowls and cover with the bread slices.

9. **Sprinkle** with the cheeses and drizzle with the remaining melted butter. Bake for 15 minutes, or until the soup is simmering and the cheese has melted. Run under a preheated broiler until the cheese is golden.

Serve at once.

When I was about ten or eleven, I got it into my head that I had to learn how to ice skate. These were the days of Sonja Henie and Tyrone Power movies. She wasn't awfully pretty, but he was a dish.

My mother agreed and promptly took herself off to Saks Fifth Avenue in New York City to purchase an appropriate outfit for her budding star. Any excuse to spend money. And money she spent. The skating costume was black velvet—a short, full skirt and a vest. What went with this, according to my mother, was a heavy, white cable-knit sweater. She'd also gotten me white figure skates just like the professionals wore.

The next Saturday I packed up my hatbox (that's what we used as a suitcase in those days) and took the subway to the Brooklyn Ice Palace on Atlantic Avenue. Even then this was considered a rough neighborhood. Lots of the kids from that neighborhood loved to skate and those kids were *reeeeally* rough!

Off I went to the ladies' lockers where I changed from my jeans into my skating outfit and ice skates. By the time I left the dressing area and walked into the arena I had quite a crowd following me. I could, after all, walk quite nimbly on the wooden floor, leading anyone to believe that I knew what I was doing. Dressed as I was like a movie star in velvet, I stood out in the crowd of casually dressed kids. They were convinced they had a real pro in their midst.

The rink was large and enclosed with a wooden fence. A waltz was playing on the loudspeaker as I delicately stepped out onto the ice. The crowds were still with me, anticipating a free ice show from Sonja Henie, Jr.

My foot immediately shot out from under me. I grabbed onto the wooden enclosure and pulled myself up. Not one of my most graceful moves. Again I tried to move and once again I fell. The fence became my support as I pulled myself around the rink, not only to the sound of the waltz, but to the hissing and booing of my former comrades. I didn't so much move on my skates as on my ankles. Who knew I had weak ankles?

After a day freezing on the rink and suffering the unpleasant remarks of my fellow skaters, I needed to get home to comfort. What could be better than a bowl of hot soup?

Great-Grandma Sadie's Potato Soup

Serves 8

3	leeks	3
4	potatoes, diced to bite-size pieces	4
1	onion, diced	1
1	shallot, diced	1
	chicken stock, homemade preferred	
1	bay leaf	1
	Kosher or coarse salt and freshly ground pepper to taste	
½ cup	all-purpose flour	125 mL
⅛–¼ cup	butter	25–50 mL
⅓ cup	chopped Italian parsley	75 mL

1. **Clean** and dice the leeks. (See Susie's Rules, page 265, for cleaning leeks.)

2. **Place** the leeks, potatoes, onion, and shallot in a large stockpot and add enough chicken stock to cover plus 1″ (2.5 cm). Add the bay leaf and the salt and pepper. Keep in mind that the stock has already been seasoned, so go easy on the salt and pepper.

3. **Cook** only until the potatoes are slightly al dente, about 20 minutes.

4. **Brown** the flour in a nonstick frying pan. This process requires constant attention and stirring to ensure that the flour does not burn. Immediately after the flour is nicely tanned, add the butter, stirring until it melts. This will turn the mixture a deep and golden brown. If the flour won't brown without burning, add some more butter to the pan.

5. When the roux is nicely browned, **stir** in a bit of the potato broth to thin the flour mixture. Then add this mixture to the stockpot, stirring constantly to ensure no lumps are formed.

6. **Heat** through to cook the flour.

Top with the chopped parsley when serving.

Jane's Sweet Pea Soup

Serves 8

1 Tbsp	butter	15 mL
1	onion, diced	1
3	garlic cloves, minced	3
3	shallots, diced	3
1	leek, diced	1
3½ lbs	fresh peas (in the shell), or 1 lb (500 g) frozen peas	1.75 kg
2	Yukon gold potatoes, diced	2
4 cups	chicken stock, homemade preferred	1 L
1 cup	heavy (35%) cream	250 mL
	Juice of 1 lemon	
1 Tbsp	kosher or coarse salt and freshly ground pepper to taste	15 mL
8 Tbsp	sour cream	100 mL
2 tsp	finely minced fresh tarragon	10 mL

1. **Melt** the butter in a stockpot. Add the diced onion, garlic, diced shallots, and diced leek, and sauté until translucent.

2. **Add** the shelled peas, diced potatoes, and hot stock to this mixture and simmer over medium heat until the potatoes are tender, about 10 minutes. Test the potatoes for doneness with a fork.

3. **Purée** the soup in a blender in batches. Pour the soup back into the stockpot and add the cream. Heat just to the boil.

4. **Add** the lemon juice and season with salt and pepper. The soup can be frozen at this point. See page 21 for tips on freezing soup.

5. **Top** each soup bowl with 1 tablespoon (15 mL) of the sour cream and a generous pinch of the tarragon.

I first tasted this soup at the Hotel Bel-Air in Los Angeles. There's nothing like a grand hotel. This one is intimate and secluded. You can dine al fresco and be served attentively and deliciously.

I loved the tortilla soup I once tasted there and was lucky to find the recipe in one of my cooking magazines. After making it a few times, I've come up with my own version.

Tortilla Soup

Serves 12					
12	6" (15 cm) yellow corn tortillas	12	½ cup	chopped fresh cilantro	125 mL
	Vegetable oil for frying tortillas		3	bay leaves	3
½ cup	vegetable oil	125 mL	8 cups	chicken stock, homemade preferred	2 L
1 Tbsp	ground cumin	15 mL	¼ cup	chopped fresh cilantro, for garnish	50 mL
1 Tbsp	paprika	15 mL			
1 tsp	chili powder	5 mL			
½ tsp	cayenne	2 mL			
½ tsp	ground coriander	2 mL			
¼ cup	leek, white part only	50 mL			
2 cups	chopped onion	500 mL			
¼ cup	chopped celery	50 mL			
6	garlic cloves, chopped	6			
4 cups	chopped tomatoes (about 3 lb/1.5 kg)	1 L			
¼ cup	canned tomato purée	50 mL			

For the tortillas:

1. **Cut** the tortillas into ¼" (5 mm) strips.

2. **Heat** about ½" (1 cm) of the oil in a large skillet over moderate heat until hot and fry the tortilla strips in batches, stirring occasionally, until pale golden and crisp, about 1 minute. Transfer the strips to paper towels to drain.

3. **Set** aside a quarter of the strips for garnish.

For the soup:

4. **Heat** the ½ cup (125 mL) of vegetable oil in a large stockpot. Add three-quarters of the fried tortilla

strips. Season with the cumin, paprika, chili powder, cayenne, and coriander and cook over moderate heat, stirring frequently, about 5 minutes or until the seasoning covers the strips.

5. **Clean** and chop the leek. (See "Susie's Rules," page 265, for cleaning leeks.)

6. **Add** the leek, onion, celery, and garlic to the pot and cook, stirring frequently, about 3 minutes.

7. **Stir** in the tomatoes, tomato purée, cilantro, bay leaves, and stock.

8. **Bring** the soup to a boil and simmer, covered, for 1 hour.

9. When slightly cool, **mix** in a blender until smooth.

10. **Reheat** the soup before serving and garnish with the crisped tortillas and chopped cilantro.

Ellen's Corn Chowder

Serves 8

2	small leeks, white part only	2
4 Tbsp	butter	50 mL
1 cup	diced onion	250 mL
1	carrot, finely diced	1
½ cup	finely diced celery	125 mL
4 cups	chicken stock, homemade preferred	1 L
1 cup	white wine	250 mL
1	bay leaf	1
1	garlic clove, minced	1
5 sprigs	fresh thyme	5 sprigs
6 ears	fresh sweet corn, shucked, kernels removed (keep the cobs)	6 ears
1½ cups	heavy cream	375 mL
	Kosher or coarse salt and freshly ground pepper to taste	
	Juice of ½ lemon	

Hot pepper cream:

½ cup	heavy (35%) cream, whipped	125 mL
¼ cup	sour cream	50 mL
1	jalapeno pepper, cored, seeded, and minced	1
3 Tbsp	chopped cilantro	45 mL
	Kosher or coarse salt and freshly ground pepper to taste	
	Fresh lemon juice	

For the soup:

1. **Clean** and dice the leeks. (See "Susie's Rules," page 265, for cleaning leeks.)

2. **Melt** the butter in a large stockpot and sauté the leeks and onions over medium heat for 10 minutes, until translucent.

3. **Add** the carrot and celery and cook for 10 minutes.

4. **Stir** in the stock, white wine, bay leaf, garlic, and thyme and bring to a boil.

5. **Add** the corncobs and the kernels and simmer for 25 to 30 minutes, or until the corn is al dente.

6. **Remove** the cobs and purée the soup in a blender in batches. The blender will give the finest purée of any of your machines.

7. **Return** the soup to the pot and add the cream.

8. **Stir** in the salt, pepper, and lemon juice.

9. **Bring** to a simmer for 1 minute.

For the hot pepper cream:

10. Just before serving, **combine** the whipped cream, sour cream, pepper, cilantro, salt, pepper, and lemon juice.

Serve the soup hot and garnish with a large spoonful of the hot pepper cream.

My mother, second from the right, with her pals at Coney Island, in the 1920s.

Many years ago, I was introduced by friends to a beautiful and incredibly forceful woman. Stunning on sight, assertive with each breath. We made small talk for a while, and then she asked me what I did.

"I'm a marketing consultant, in the real estate field," I said.

"You WILL call my daughter! She's a real estate lawyer and you two should know each other."

"Okay," I agreed, merely to end the discussion.

About two weeks later my phone rang. "Hi, I'm Audrey," the voice said. "You met my mother and she told you to call me. She's an outrageous woman, so I knew you'd never make the call. So here I am."

Audrey's only like her mother in that she's wonderfully assertive, but not outrageous at all. She's married to a dear and gentle Scotsman who every now and then says, "Audrey, stop it. People will think you're serious." And serious she is.

Audrey is one of the few women I know who makes me look passive. I love her so for that. I know too well that underneath her bold exterior lives a sensitive, giving, and loving friend.

Audrey's Tomato Soup

Serves 8, or you can double and freeze for future use		
2 Tbsp	olive oil	25 mL
1	onion, diced	1
2 tsp	chopped garlic	10 mL
1 cup	chopped dill	250 mL
2	cans (28 oz/796 mL) Italian plum tomatoes	2
6 cups	V8 juice	1.5 L
4 Tbsp	powdered chicken bouillon (soup base)	50 mL
2 tsp	seasoned salt	10 mL
½ cup	heavy (35%) cream	125 mL
	Kosher or coarse salt and freshly ground pepper to taste	

1. **Sauté** the onions and garlic in the oil in a stock-pot until golden. Be careful not to burn the garlic.

2. **Add** the dill, tomatoes, V8 juice, bouillon, and seasoned salt. Cook for 30 minutes.

3. **Slowly add** the cream.

4. **Season** with salt and pepper to taste.

5. **Purée** in a blender until smooth. Reheat and serve.

The soup can be served hot or cold.

If we were really organized we'd make batches of this soup in season and freeze for a cold winter's day.

Trudy's Summer Tomato Soup

Serves 8		
3 lbs	fresh tomatoes, cored and cut into quarters	1.5 kg
8	garlic cloves	8
3	large shallots	3
3 sprigs	fresh rosemary or ¼ tsp (1 mL) dried rosemary	3 sprigs
1 Tbsp	chopped fresh thyme or 1 tsp (5 mL) dried thyme	15 mL
⅔ cup	olive oil	150 mL
1	large onion, diced	1
1	garlic clove, minced	1
2	celery stalks, diced	2
3	carrots peeled, trimmed, and diced	3
4 cups	chicken stock, homemade preferred	1 L
2 tsp	fresh basil	10 mL
	Kosher or coarse salt and freshly ground pepper to taste	
¼ tsp	granulated sugar	1 mL

1. **Preheat** the oven to 400° F (200° C)

2. **Put** the tomatoes, garlic, shallots, rosemary, and thyme in a lightly greased 9″ × 11″ (22 cm × 28 cm) ovenproof baking dish. Cover with ½ cup (125 mL) of the olive oil.

3. **Bake** until the tomatoes are lightly browned, 20 to 25 minutes.

4. **Heat** the remaining 2 tablespoons of olive oil over medium high heat in a 4-quart (4 L) heated stockpot. Add the onion and minced garlic and cook until translucent, about 5 minutes.

5. **Add** the celery and carrots (this is now a *mirepoix*, the basis of most great sauces and soups). Cook for 10 to 15 minutes.

6. **Transfer** the tomato mixture and half the liquid from the baking dish to the stockpot, using a slotted spoon.

Here I am—Susie at three.

7. **Chiffonade** the basil. (See "Susie's Rules," page 264, for instructions on chiffonade.)

8. **Add** the chicken stock, basil, salt, pepper, and sugar and simmer for about 15 minutes, or until the liquids have reduced by about one third.

9. **Purée** the soup in a blender. Strain through a medium strainer.

Serve hot.

I was in Paris recently and had dinner at L'Amboisie, my favorite restaurant in the world. They served their gazpacho very, very well puréed with a dab of cream mixed into the soup. It was the color of a pink peony and very delicious. For my recipe, I've done the soup in chunky fashion, but you might like to try it à L'Amboisie. Just purée the ingredients a bit longer.

Gazpacho

Serves 8 to 10		
2	sweet red peppers	2
2	medium onions	2
2	large shallots	2
2	large cucumbers	2
6	large, ripe tomatoes	6

Juice mixture:

½ cup	red wine vinegar	125 mL
½ cup	olive oil	125 mL
1½ cups	canned tomato juice	375 mL
3	eggs, lightly beaten	3
½ cup	chopped fresh dill	125 mL
	Kosher or coarse salt and freshly ground pepper to taste	
Pinch	cayenne pepper	Pinch

1. **Core,** seed, and coarsely chop the peppers.

2. **Peel** and coarsely chop the onions and shallots.

3. **Peel,** seed, and coarsely chop the cucumbers.

4. **Peel,** seed, and coarsely chop the tomatoes, saving the juice. (See "Susie's Rules," page 267, for peeling tomatoes.)

5. **Whisk** together the vinegar, olive oil, reserved tomato juice, canned tomato juice, and eggs in a small bowl.

6. **Purée** the vegetables, individually, in small batches, in a food processor fitted with a steel blade, adding the juice mixture as necessary to keep the blades from clogging. Do not purée completely—the gazpacho should retain some of its crunchiness.

7. **Put** the vegetables and their juices in a large bowl and combine with the remaining juice mixture.

8. **Add** the dill, salt, and cayenne pepper to taste.

9. **Cover** and chill for at least 4 hours.

This is one of my favorite summer soups. I love going out to my vegetable garden to pick the leeks and then to the herb garden to cut the fresh chives. How did a little girl from Brooklyn come to this?

Vichyssoise

Serves 8

3 cups	leeks, white part only to ensure the soup is white and not green	750 mL
¼ cup	butter	50 mL
1	onion, diced	1
5	medium Yukon gold or russet potatoes, diced	5
1 Tbsp	kosher or coarse salt	15 mL
	Freshly ground pepper to taste	
2 quarts	chicken stock, homemade preferred	2 L
1 cup	heavy (35%) cream	250 mL
½ cup	chopped chives	125 mL

1. **Clean** and slice the leeks. (See "Susie's Rules," page 265, for cleaning leeks.)

2. **Melt** the butter in a stockpot and add the onion and leeks. Cover the pan and cook over low heat for about 5 minutes to steam the onions. Then remove the cover and continue cooking over low heat for another 10 minutes, being careful not to brown the vegetables, but rather to ensure they are softened.

3. **Add** the potatoes, salt, pepper, and stock to the pot. Simmer gently until the vegetables are tender, about 20 to 30 minutes more, depending on the size of the potatoes.

4. **Purée** the slightly cooled soup in a blender in batches until you have removed any lumps. I strain out about half of the liquid and purée the remainder with the vegetables. I then add the liquid to the potatoes, gently stirring. I do this to ensure that the soup is not too thick. Works well.

5. **Add** the cream to the mixture and refrigerate until serving. Before serving, check for seasoning.

Serve the soup cold and garnish with chopped chives.

Salads

Salads were never a part of my childhood. Sometimes, maybe, you'd get a wedge of iceberg lettuce and a slice of tomato. Arugula? Never! Endive? You've got to be kidding.

Today's salads are a way of testing your creativity. You can put good vinaigrette on just about anything and it will taste good. Apples, oranges, and even nuts have eased their way into our salad vocabulary.

I am terribly lazy when it comes to making salad. The washing, the rinsing, and the drying are a bit of a drag for me. But when company comes, I go all out. Here are some of my favorites.

Nothing is better than the combination of beets and goat cheese, especially when the beets are just picked.

Beet Mille Feuille Salad

Serves 8

8	beets	8
6 oz	goat cheese, at room temperature	170 g
	Heavy (35%) cream	
	Kosher or coarse salt and freshly ground pepper to taste	
	Lettuce	
	Simple Vinaigrette (see page 68)	

Preheat oven to 450°F (230°C)

1. **Remove** the greens from beets, leaving 2″ (5 cm) at the top for flavor. Wash and wrap each beet in foil. Depending on the size of the beet, bake for 1 hour, or until cooked. Test with a fork for doneness.

2. **Remove** the foil. Cut off the green and tail of the beet. The beet skin can now be removed with your fingertips. Cool and cover.

3. **Whip** the goat cheese with a bit of heavy cream to soften.

4. **Season** with salt and pepper to taste.

5. **Slice** each beet about $1/8$″ (3 mm) thin. I try to round each slice with a cookie cutter so that they are the same size. Spread each slice with the goat cheese, creating a tower of beet slices and cheese.

Serve on a bed of lettuce that has been tossed with vinaigrette.

This salad is not only delicious, it makes a beautiful presentation. You'll need a large platter, over 12" (30.5 cm) long, that's at least 1" (2.5 cm) deep.

Liz's Cobb Salad

Serves 6 to 8

Dressing:

⅓ cup	red wine vinegar	75 mL
	Kosher or coarse salt and freshly ground pepper to taste	
2 tsp	fresh lemon juice	10 mL
½ tsp	Dijon mustard	2 mL
1	small garlic clove, minced	1
1 cup	olive oil	250 mL
2 Tbsp	chopped fresh chives	25 mL
1 Tbsp	chopped Italian parsley	15 mL

Chicken:

2	boneless, skinless chicken breasts	2
1 sprig	thyme	1 sprig
1 sprig	Italian parsley	1 sprig
1	celery stalk	1
1 Tbsp	kosher or coarse salt	15 mL
½ tsp	freshly ground pepper	2 mL
1	bay leaf	1

Salad:

½ head	romaine lettuce, washed	½ head
½ head	Bibb lettuce, washed	½ head
½ bunch	watercress, washed and coarsely chopped	½ bunch
2	medium tomatoes	2
6 slices	bacon, fried, drained, and crumbled	6 slices
4	hard-boiled eggs, peeled and quartered	4
1	avocado, pitted, peeled, and diced	1
¾ cup	Roquefort cheese, crumbled	175 mL

For the dressing:

1. **Mix** together the vinegar, salt, and pepper in a small bowl.

2. **Add** the lemon juice, mustard, and garlic.

3. **Whisk** in the olive oil.

4. **Add** the chives and parsley. Set aside.

For the chicken:

5. **Place** the chicken in a saucepan with the thyme, parsley, celery, salt, pepper, and bay leaf. Add enough water to cover and place over medium heat.

6. **Bring** to a boil and skim off any foam that rises to the top. Reduce the heat to low and cover. Simmer for about 20 minutes or until the chicken juices run clear. Cool the chicken and dice. Set aside.

For the salad:

7. **Stack** the romaine lettuce and cut across into strips about 1″ (2.5 cm) wide.

8. **Break** the Bibb lettuce into chunks.

9. **Arrange** the romaine, Bibb, and watercress on the serving platter.

10. **Peel,** core, seed, and dice the tomatoes. (See "Susie's Rules," page 267, for peeling tomatoes.)

11. **Place** the tomatoes in a strip down the center, then arrange the chicken, bacon, eggs, avocado, and Roquefort in strips on either side of the tomatoes.

12. **Pour** the dressing over the salad and serve immediately.

Coleslaw

Serves 6		
½	green cabbage, thinly shredded (You can use a food processor or a knife.)	½
2	carrots, peeled and grated	2
1 cup	mayonnaise	250 mL
5–7 Tbsp	white wine, or champagne vinegar, or herb vinegar (see page 250)	75–100 mL
3 tsp	hot horseradish	15 mL
½ cup	sour cream	125 mL
1 tsp	celery seed	5 mL
1 tsp	granulated sugar	5 mL
	Kosher or coarse salt and freshly ground pepper to taste	
½ cup	chopped Italian parsley	125 mL

1. **Put** the cabbage and carrots in a large bowl.

2. **Mix** the mayonnaise, vinegar, horseradish, sour cream, celery seed, and sugar in a medium bowl.

3. **Pour** the dressing over the cabbage mixture and toss to coat.

4. **Season** to taste with salt and pepper.

5. **Taste** to adjust the vinegar—I find I am always adding more.

6. **Sprinkle** the coleslaw with the parsley and serve.

Coleslaw can be prepared 4 hours ahead. Cover and refrigerate.

This dish is authentically Hungarian—it comes to me direct from Hungary, from the mother of my friend, Emilia. Her mother and I have rarely been alone together since conversation between us would be totally impossible. She does not speak one word of English and I speak no Hungarian. Emilia translates. However, this dish proves that good food is understood everywhere.

Hungarian Cucumber Salad

Serves 6 to 8

2	large cucumbers (about 2 lbs/1 kg)	2
1 Tbsp	kosher or coarse salt	15 mL
1/3 cup	white wine vinegar	75 mL
2 tsp	granulated sugar	10 mL
1	garlic clove, minced	1
1 tsp	dill seed	5 mL
1/4 cup	water	50 mL
2 tsp	chopped fresh dill	10 mL

1. If using seedless cucumbers, **score** lengthwise with a fork before slicing. If using regular cucumbers, peel and seed. I find using the tip of a teaspoon works best to get all of the seeds out.

2. **Slice** the cucumbers very, very thinly using a mandoline. Toss the slices with salt and drain for 1 hour in a colander or strainer.

3. **Bring** the vinegar, sugar, garlic, dill seed, and water to a boil in a small saucepan, stirring until the sugar is dissolved. Cool.

4. **Drain** the cucumbers and rinse very well under cold water to remove all of the salt. Drain and pat dry so that the cukes can accept the dressing.

5. **Combine** the cucumbers with the dressing and chopped dill, and marinate, covered, then refrigerate for at least 1 hour and up to 6 hours.

Agreat summer lunch to eat al fresco. One of the best parts of this salad is the presentation—a large, beautiful platter no less than 1" (2.5 cm) deep is required for serving.

Salad Niçoise

Serves 6 to 8

Green beans:

2 Tbsp	kosher or coarse salt	25 mL
2 lbs	French green beans, stem end removed	1 kg

Potato salad:

1½ lbs	baby new potatoes or Yukon Gold potatoes	750 g
2 Tbsp	kosher or coarse salt	25 mL
6 Tbsp or more	tarragon vinegar (you need to taste the salad to adjust for tartness)	90 mL or more
1 tsp	Dijon mustard	4 mL
1	garlic clove, minced	1
9 Tbsp	olive oil	135 mL
	Kosher or coarse salt and freshly ground pepper to taste	
1½ tsp	finely minced shallot	8 mL

Dressing:

1½ tsp	Dijon mustard	8 mL
	Kosher or coarse salt and freshly ground pepper to taste	
¼ cup	fresh lemon juice	50 mL
½ cup	olive oil	125 mL
1½ tsp	finely minced shallot	8 mL
1	green leaf lettuce, rinsed and spun dry	1

Salad:

1 large head	Boston lettuce, leaves separated, rinsed, and spun dry	1 large head
4	red tomatoes, quartered	4
1	red onion, thinly sliced	1
1	red pepper, cored and thinly sliced	1
6	hard-boiled eggs (I put my eggs in a saucepan covered with cold water and time for 20 minutes.)	6

10 oz	chunk white tuna (It is important to get only the best imported, preferably Italian, tuna.)	300 g
	Freshly ground pepper to taste	
1	can or jar (2 oz/50 g) anchovy fillets packed in olive oil	1
Handful	French black olives, Niçoise preferred	Handful

For the green beans:

1. **Bring** 10 quarts (10 L) of water to a boil in a large saucepan. Add salt and the beans. Cover and return to the boil. Cook for about 4 minutes. The beans should be cooked until just tender with the slightest crunch. Drain immediately.

2. **Place** the beans in a basin of ice water to cool while you prepare the potatoes and dressing. When they are chilled, drain, pat dry, and toss with just enough dressing to lightly coat, and then refrigerate.

For the potato salad:

3. If you are using baby potatoes, **wash** them well. If you are using Yukon's, peel and cut them into bite-size pieces before cooking. Bring the potatoes to a boil in salted water, uncovered, for about 20 minutes, or until cooked through. Taste to check.

4. While the potatoes are cooking, **combine** the vinegar, mustard, and garlic in a small bowl.

5. Gradually **whisk** in the oil.

6. **Season** with salt and freshly ground pepper.

7. **Add** the shallot.

8. **Drain** the potatoes well and put them into a large bowl. If you are using baby potatoes, cut them into bite-size pieces after they are cooked.

(continues on page 54)

9. **Pour** this oil and vinegar mixture over the cooked and still hot potatoes, gently tossing them. Taste for seasoning. Toss several times as the potatoes cool.

For the dressing:

10. **Mix** the Dijon, salt, and pepper with a fork until well mixed, and then add the lemon juice.

11. **Slowly add** the olive oil and whisk until well combined, and then add the shallot.

Assemble the salad:

12. When ready to serve, **toss** the lettuce, tomato, onion, and pepper in a large bowl with just enough dressing to coat.

13. **Quarter** the eggs lengthwise and put aside.

14. **Drain** and flake the tuna and season it with pepper.

15. **Arrange** the lettuce, tomato, onion and pepper mixture on a large beautiful platter.

16. **Taste** for seasoning, adding more lemon juice, salt, and pepper if needed.

17. **Pile** the potato salad in the center of the platter.

18. **Divide** the beans into six sections and place them around the edge of the platter.

19. **Arrange** the eggs on the edges of the platter to alternate with the beans.

20. **Sprinkle** the anchovies, black olives, and tuna over the vegetables. Serve immediately.

Roasted Pear Salad

Serves 4

4	firm Bartlett pears	4
1 Tbsp	butter, melted	15 mL
1 Tbsp	granulated sugar	15 mL
1 cup	walnuts, chopped coarsely and roasted	250 mL

Vinaigrette:

⅓ cup	olive oil	75 mL
2 Tbsp	white wine vinegar or herb vinegar (see page 250)	25 mL
	Kosher or coarse salt and freshly ground black pepper to taste	

Salad:

1	small Boston lettuce	1
1 bunch	arugula, rinsed and dried, hard stems removed and torn into bite-size pieces	1 bunch
4 oz	Parmigiano-Reggiano cheese, shaved into thin strips with vegetable peeler	125 g

Preheat the oven to 500°F (260°C)

1. **Peel** and halve each pear lengthwise and remove the core.
2. **Slice** the pear into eight pieces.
3. **Gently toss** the pears with the melted butter.
4. **Add** the sugar and toss again to combine.
5. **Spread** the pears in single layer on a silpat- or parchment-lined baking sheet. Roast with the rack in middle of the oven until browned, about 10 minutes.
6. **Turn** each slice and roast until golden brown for about 5 minutes more. Let the pears cool. The pears can be roasted up to 3 hours in advance and kept at room temperature.
7. **Roast** the walnuts in the oven until lightly browned and fragrant, about 3 minutes. Watch carefully, they burn quite quickly. I usually put the timer on so that I won't forget them.

For the vinaigrette:

8. **Whisk** together the olive oil, vinegar, salt, and pepper in small bowl.

For the salad:

9. **Toss** the lettuces with the vinaigrette. Distribute the greens on four salad plates and top with the pears and Parmigiano-Reggiano slices. Sprinkle with the chopped walnuts and serve immediately.

New Potato Salad with Herbs and Shallots

Serves 12

Vinaigrette:

1 tsp	Dijon mustard	5 mL
1	garlic clove, minced	1
6 Tbsp or more	tarragon or herb vinegar (see page 250). You need to taste the dressing to adjust for tartness.	90 mL or more
9 Tbsp	olive oil	135 mL
	Kosher or coarse salt and freshly ground pepper to taste	

Salad:

6 lbs	new potatoes	3 kg
2 Tbsp	kosher or coarse salt	25 mL
4	shallots, minced	4
1 cup	diced celery	250 mL
1 cup	chopped green onions	250 mL
1 cup	mayonnaise	250 mL
¼ cup	chopped fresh dill	50 mL
¼ cup	minced Italian parsley	50 mL
3 Tbsp	chopped chives	45 mL

For the vinaigrette:

1. **Combine** the mustard, garlic, and vinegar, in a bowl.
2. **Gradually whisk** in the oil and season with the salt and pepper.

For the salad:

3. **Wash** the potatoes. Cover the potatoes with salted water in a large pot and bring to the boil. Cook until the potatoes are just tender. Tasting them is the only way to ensure that the potatoes have reached the proper consistency.
4. **Drain** the water and slice the warm potatoes into bite-size pieces.
5. **Place** them in a large bowl and toss them with the vinaigrette and shallots. Let this mixture stand for 30 minutes, gently tossing every now and then to ensure that the dressing covers all the potatoes.
6. **Mix** the celery, green onions, mayonnaise, dill, parsley, and chives into the potatoes, being careful not to break the potatoes down.
7. **Taste** for seasoning, cover, and refrigerate. Can be prepared 1 day ahead.

Serve at room temperature.

Tomato Salad with Shallot Dressing

Serves 4		
1 lb	tomatoes	500 g
	Kosher or coarse salt and freshly ground pepper to taste	
3 Tbsp	balsamic vinegar	45 mL
1 Tbsp	granulated sugar	15 mL
3 Tbsp	olive oil	45 mL
1 tsp	Dijon mustard	5 mL
2	shallots, minced	2
2 Tbsp	fresh basil	25 mL
2 Tbsp	finely chopped fresh oregano	25 mL

1. **Slice** or halve the tomatoes.
2. **Season** with salt and pepper.
3. **Whisk** together the vinegar, sugar, olive oil, mustard, and shallots.
4. **Chiffonade** the basil. (See "Susie's Rules," page 264.)
5. **Drizzle** the dressing over the tomatoes and sprinkle with the oregano and basil.

Caesar Salad

Serves 4

2 heads	romaine lettuce	2 heads
3	small garlic cloves, minced	3
3	flat anchovy fillets, drained and minced	3
2	large egg yolks	2
1½ tsp	fresh lemon juice	7 mL
1½ tsp	Dijon mustard	7 mL
1 Tbsp	white wine vinegar	15 mL
2 tsp	balsamic vinegar	10 mL
	Kosher or coarse salt and freshly ground pepper to taste	
¾ cup	olive oil	175 mL

Garlic croutons:

2	large garlic cloves, minced	2
2 Tbsp	butter	25 mL
1 cup	French or Italian bread, cut in ½" (1 cm) cubes	250 mL
	Kosher or coarse salt to taste	
¼ cup	freshly grated Parmigiano-Reggiano cheese	50 mL

1. **Wash** the leaves of the lettuce and spin dry. I hate to be wasteful, but the outer leaves of the romaine are often too tough and should be discarded. Stack the leaves and cut across in a 1″ (2.5 cm) slice. Set aside.

For the dressing:

2. **Mash** the minced garlic and anchovies to form a paste.

3. **Mix** together the paste, yolks, lemon juice, mustard, vinegars, salt, and pepper.

4. **Slowly add** the oil in a stream, whisking the dressing until it becomes emulsified.

Preheat the oven to 350°F (180°C)

For the croutons:

5. **Cook** the garlic in the butter in a small skillet with an ovenproof handle over a moderately low heat, stirring, for 5 minutes. Add the bread cubes and cook the croutons, tossing them, until they are lightly coated with the garlic butter.

6. **Bake** for about 10 minutes, tossing the pan several times, until the croutons are nicely browned. Sprinkle the croutons with salt to taste and transfer them to paper towels to drain. Makes about 1 cup (250 mL).

7. **Toss** the romaine with the dressing in a wooden salad bowl when just ready to serve, tossing the salad until it is well combined.

8. **Toss** the grated cheese and croutons into the salad. Taste before serving to adjust seasoning, as required.

Greek Salad

Serves 4

Vinaigrette:

1/3 cup	olive oil	75 mL
1 Tbsp	chopped shallots	15 mL
2 tsp	grated lemon zest	10 mL
2½ Tbsp	fresh lemon juice	35 mL
1 heaping Tbsp	chopped fresh oregano	20 mL
	Kosher or coarse salt and freshly ground pepper to taste	

Salad:

1	cucumber	1
1	small red pepper	1
1	red onion	1
1 lb	tomatoes (in season) or cherry tomatoes	500 g
1	Bibb or iceberg lettuce, washed and spun dry	1
½ lb	feta cheese, crumbled	250 g
12	black Greek olives	12

For the vinaigrette:

1. **Combine** the olive oil, shallots, lemon zest, lemon juice, oregano, salt, and pepper in a bowl.

For the salad:

2. If using seedless cucumbers, **score** lengthwise with a fork and thinly slice. If using regular cucumbers, peel and seed. I find using the tip of a teaspoon works best to get all of the seeds out. Cut into bite-size pieces.

3. **Cut** the red pepper into bite-size pieces.

4. **Slice** the red onion very thin.

5. **Quarter** the tomatoes.

6. **Break** the lettuce into bite-size pieces.

7. **Toss** all the vegetables in a large bowl with the vinaigrette, and add the cheese and olives.

Halina's Oriental Salad

½ cup	slivered almonds	125 mL
6 Tbsp	sesame seeds	90 mL
4 packages	Ramen noodles, chicken-flavored or plain	4 packages

Dressing:

4 packets	Ramen soup seasoning	4 packets
1 cup	peanut oil	250 mL
2 Tbsp	granulated sugar	25 mL
9 Tbsp	white vinegar	135 mL
	Kosher or coarse salt and freshly ground pepper to taste	
3 Tbsp	sesame oil	45 mL

Salad:

7 cups	cabbage	1.75 L
12	green onions, chopped	12

Preheat the oven to 350°F (180°C)

1. **Toast** the almonds and then the sesame seeds in the oven, being careful that they do not burn. Do not toast the nuts and seeds together as their cooking times vary.

2. **Remove** the seasoning packets from the Ramen soup packages and crunch the noodles in their bags into pieces about 1" (2.5) long.

For the dressing:

3. **Combine** the Ramen soup seasoning, peanut oil, sugar, vinegar, salt, pepper, and sesame oil to make the dressing. The dressing can be made a day before; whisk it again just before serving.

For the salad:

4. **Shred** the cabbage, which can be then be stored for 1 day in a sealed plastic bag until ready to serve. You can use a food processor or a knife for this job.

5. **Toss** the cabbage with the dressing.

6. **Add** the Raman noodles, almonds, sesame seeds, and green onions and serve at once.

If we're blessed, we have old, dear friends who know us and accept us as we are. My friend Ellen is one of those people. I met her when I was sixteen and we were both attending summer school at the Cornell University campus.

Ellen came from "the city," one of three daughters in a very wealthy family. Everything that she needed was provided for her, except for a loving mother. For this, she came to my house in Brooklyn. These trips were

My dear friend Ellen and me.

an adventure for her. We had no cook, no butler, no maid—it was just a madhouse and she loved every minute of it.

Ellen is the most nurturing person I've ever known. She's one of the few people in my life I can allow to do me a favor without feeling too guilty.

After fourteen unhappy years in my first marriage, I finally found the courage to separate from my husband. This was 1970, when very few women left marriages. There were no support groups, and I didn't know any sympathetic recently divorced or single women to speak to. There was no one to turn to, to advise me. I was living in Toronto at the time, while my family was still back in Brooklyn. I was quite alone and terrified.

To prepare myself for my new life as a divorcée, I'd started to work a year before the separation. I knew I would need the money to help support my three small children. So now I was mother, homemaker, budding career woman, and lunatic—rushing, running, and just plain scared. I hadn't been here before and just didn't know anything else to do but try to hang in and make my kids feel safe. I had no money, lots of fear and doubt, and few friends who understood what I was going through. Except for Ellen. She knew exactly how I felt and how to make me feel better, effortlessly.

Ellen and her husband would invite my little family to their house in Long Island every summer for three weeks so we'd have some semblance of a holiday. I'd pack the car, prepare the kids, and drive from Toronto to New York. I felt like a woman on a mission during those 12-hour drives, going straight through without a stop. The children sensed the difficulty of the hard drive and, miraculously, behaved like angels until we were off the highway and onto Ellen's driveway.

So Liz, Andy, Owen, and I, and Ellen and her three children, Beth, Jed, and Gil, would create our own three-week-long "summer camp." And what a camp it was! Before we were up in the morning, Ellen would have already gone for fresh, hot bagels, done my laundry, and made breakfast. Then it was off to the beach, where we would spend the days with our six children, who would all at once be in the pool, the ocean, eating, staring, and loving each other.

Who in her right mind would take in a family of four but my friend Ellen? She is the sister I never had—-and, to this day, is still one of my dearest friends.

This is Ellen's fabulous Moroccan salad—another of her many gifts to me.

Ellen's Moroccan Hot Salad

Serves 6 to 8		
20	cherry tomatoes, diced, or 6 large tomatoes, diced	20
3	red peppers, diced	3
6	green onions, diced	6
2 to 4	hot cherry peppers, cut into "teeny weenie" pieces (those are Ellen's words)	2 to 4
1	bunch celery, diced	1
½ cup	chopped Italian parsley	125 mL
4	whole lemons (juice and pulp, but no seeds)	4
2 Tbsp	olive oil	25 mL
½ cup	capers	125 mL
	Kosher or coarse salt and freshly ground pepper to taste	

1. **Mix** all the vegetables and the parsley together in a large bowl.
2. **Add** the lemon juice, olive oil, capers, salt, and pepper.

You can prepare this lovely tart dish 4 to 6 hours before serving.

Sautéed Mushrooms with Greens

4 servings		
1 cup	leeks, white part only	250 mL
½ cup	walnut oil or olive oil	125 mL
¾ lb	mixed mushrooms, such as shiitake, oyster, portobello, or white mushrooms, sliced	375 mL
1 Tbsp	fresh lemon juice	15 mL
1	garlic clove, minced	1
1 Tbsp	dry sherry	15 mL
2 Tbsp	chopped Italian parsley	25 mL
1 tsp	sherry wine vinegar	5 mL
1 tsp	Dijon mustard	5 mL
¼ tsp	caraway seeds	1 mL
4 cups	assorted greens	1 L
½ cup	Simple Vinaigrette (see page 68)	125 mL

1. **Clean** and slice the leeks. (See Susie's Rules, page 265, for cleaning leeks.)

2. **Heat** the oil in large hot skillet. Add the leeks and sauté until softened, about 5 minutes.

3. **Add** the mushrooms, lemon juice, and garlic and sauté until tender, about 5 minutes.

4. **Add** the sherry and bring to a boil. Set the mushrooms aside.

5. **Combine** the parsley, sherry wine vinegar, mustard, and caraway seeds in the same skillet and whisk to blend.

6. **Toss** the mushrooms into the mustard mixture.

7. **Toss** the greens with the vinaigrette and then divide onto four plates. Top with the warm mushroom mixture and serve.

Baked Goat Cheese with Salad

Serves 4		
2" log	goat cheese	5 cm log
¼ cup	olive oil	50 mL
	Additional olive oil for oiling the dish	
5 sprigs	fresh thyme	5 sprigs
2	bay leaves, crumbled	2
½ tsp	kosher or coarse salt and freshly ground pepper to taste	2 mL
½ cup	fine dry bread crumbs (see page 247)	125 mL
5 cups	fresh greens	1.25 L
½ cup	Simple Vinaigrette (see page 68)	125 mL

1. **Slice** the goat cheese log into four ¹/₂″ (1 cm) disks using a sharp, wet knife.

2. **Combine** olive oil with the thyme, bay leaves, salt, and pepper in a shallow dish.

3. **Carefully dunk** the cheese disks into the marinade, turning them to coat on both sides. Marinate in the refrigerator, covered, for several hours or overnight.

4. **Remove** the goat cheese from the oil and coat with the bread crumbs, pressing the crumbs onto the cheese.

5. **Put** the cheese on a parchment- or silpat-lined baking dish and chill until firm, about 1 hour.

Preheat the oven to 450°F (230°C)

6. **Bake** cheese in the preheated oven until it is bubbling and golden brown, about 5 minutes.

7. **Toss** the greens with the vinaigrette and divide among four plates.

8. **Place** a round of warm goat cheese on the center of each salad, brown side up and serve immediately.

This dressing is best served the simplest way. Cut one head of iceberg lettuce into four wedges. Wash and drain very, very well. The better the blue cheese you use, the better the dressing will be. The choice is yours.

Blue Cheese Salad Dressing

Serves 4 (you can cut the recipe in half for 2)

1 cup	sour cream	250 mL
1 cup	mayonnaise	250 mL
1 tsp	minced garlic	5 mL
1/2 tsp	Worcestershire sauce	2 mL
3 Tbsp	white wine vinegar or herb vinegar (see page 250)	45 mL
	Kosher or coarse salt and freshly ground pepper to taste	
1/2 cup	blue cheese, crumbled	125 mL
1/2 cup	chopped Italian parsley	125 mL

1. **Mix** together the sour cream, mayonnaise, garlic, Worcestershire sauce, and vinegar.

2. **Season** with salt and pepper to taste.

3. **Add** the cheese and chopped parsley when ready to serve.

4. **Pour** over the wedges of lettuce.

This is a great, easy and quick alternative to a Caesar dressing

Garlic-Parmesan Dressing

Makes 1⅓ cups of dressing		
2	garlic cloves, minced	2
1 tsp	kosher or coarse salt and freshly ground pepper to taste	5 mL
⅓ cup	red wine vinegar, or more to taste	75 mL
1 cup	olive oil	250 mL
¼ cup	grated Parmigiano-Reggiano cheese	50 mL

1. **Put** the minced garlic into a small bowl and sprinkle with the salt and pepper. Using the back of a wooden spoon, press and mash the salt into the garlic.

2. **Add** the vinegar.

3. **Whisk** in the olive oil.

When ready to serve, add the parmesan cheese and toss. Romaine lettuce is best.

Simple Vinaigrette

Makes just over 1 cup

1 tsp	Dijon mustard	5 mL
1 tsp	kosher or coarse salt	5 mL
¼ cup	white wine or herb vinegar (see page 250)	50 mL
1 cup	olive oil	250 mL
¼ tsp	freshly ground pepper	1 mL

1. **Put** the mustard and salt into a small mixing bowl. Combine well with a fork.

2. **Mix** the vinegar into the mustard.

3. **Add** the pepper and then slowly add the olive oil, whisking until well combined.

Voilà ... vinaigrette.

This is a favorite family salad dressing. I like to serve it with a traditional salad of iceberg lettuce, tomato, cucumber, radish, green onion and red pepper. Nothing fancy or elaborate—just good!

Grandma Jeanne's Salad Dressing

Serves 4 to 6 (can be doubled for more)

¼ cup	corn oil	50 mL
¼ cup	white vinegar	50 mL
½ cup	mayonnaise	125 mL
1 tsp	Dijon mustard	5 mL
	Kosher or coarse salt and freshly ground pepper to taste	
2	hard-boiled eggs	2

1. **Combine** all the ingredients except the eggs. Set aside.

2. When ready to serve, **chop** the eggs and add to the dressing.

3. **Toss** the salad immediately or the eggs will break down.

Eggs and Dairy

I know that too many eggs aren't good for you. That's sad. There was a time when every day you could sit down to a plate of eggs fried in butter, with crisp bacon and rye bread toast, with more butter. You'd top it off with a cold glass of milk.

Or, after a miserable day, you'd come home and scramble an egg for supper and sit by the radio, listening to a favorite show.

Eggs were the original comfort food.

I first tasted this omelet in a diner in Los Angeles. Like many of my favorite restaurants, it was a dump, but a dump with good food. I do appreciate a fine dining room, but it's always the food that gets me, not the ambiance. So here's to diner Boursin Omelet.

Boursin Omelet

Serves 2		
4	eggs	4
2 Tbsp	milk or half-and-half cream	25 mL
	Kosher or coarse salt and freshly ground pepper to taste	
1 Tbsp	butter	15 mL
½ cup	Boursin cheese, herb preferred	125 mL

1. **Whisk** the eggs with the milk, salt, and pepper in a medium bowl.

2. **Heat** the butter in a 10″ (25 cm) nonstick sauté pan. Reduce the heat to medium high, add the eggs, and let them set.

3. **Gently lift** the edges of the eggs as they cook, using a wooden spatula, allowing the uncooked egg to seep to the edge of the pan. Do not disturb the center of the omelet. Lift and tilt the pan as you go.

4. When the eggs are just about set, **crumble** the Boursin onto half of the omelet.

5. With a spatula, **fold** the other half of the omelet over the cheese.

6. **Lower** the heat and cover the pan for about 2 or 3 minutes to melt the cheese. Cut in half and serve at once.

I rarely serve brunch without offering eggs and onions. As you know by now, I like to leave as little as possible for the last minute. Ergo you will always find a bag full of well-caramelized onions in my freezer. Just break off a piece when you need it and voila!

Eggs and Onions

Serves 4		
¼ cup	butter	50 mL
6	onions, diced	6
½ Tbsp	granulated sugar	8 mL
Eggs:		
¼ cup	butter	50 mL
8	eggs, well beaten	8
	Kosher or coarse salt and freshly ground pepper to taste	

1. **Melt** butter in a large sauté pan.

2. **Add** the onions to the hot, melted butter.

3. **Cover** for 15 minutes to let the onions steam.

4. **Remove** the cover, add the sugar, and cook over low to medium heat until the onions are nicely caramelized and brown. Don't rush it. This step can take as long as 30 minutes. The onions can be frozen for later use.

5. **Prepare** eggs 2 at a time. For each pair of eggs, melt 1 tablespoon (15 mL) of the butter in a non-stick frying pan. Mix the eggs with ¼ of the onions and scramble to the desired consistency. Season with salt and pepper.

Most people I know believe that I am capable of just about anything. Yes, I am a competent and organized woman. Certainly I think I am courageous. There is little that frightens me, except the worry about the health and well-being of those I love. But a soufflé? No way would I tackle one until just this year. Senior citizen cooks soufflé!

Here's the real poop. It's easy. Serve with a salad and simple vinaigrette (page 68). Sooooo good!

Cheese Soufflé

Serves 4		
1 Tbsp	soft butter	15 mL
3 Tbsp	grated Parmigiano-Reggiano cheese	45 mL
2 Tbsp	butter	25 mL
3 Tbsp	all-purpose flour	45 mL
1 cup	hot milk (I use 2%)	250 mL
½ tsp	kosher or coarse salt	2 mL
¼ tsp	freshly ground pepper	1 mL
½ tsp	paprika	2 mL
⅛ tsp	freshly ground nutmeg	0.5 mL
1 cup	grated cheddar cheese	250 mL
1 cup	grated Swiss cheese	250 mL
4	egg yolks	4
6	egg whites, at room temperature	6

Preheat the oven to 375°F (190°C)

1. **Heavily butter** an 8" (2 L) round soufflé dish.

2. **Sprinkle** the Parmigiano-Reggiano cheese around the sides and the bottom of the dish.

3. **Make** a collar for the dish—in order to help the soufflé rise—by buttering a double thickness of foil that will stick up from the top of the dish about 3" (8 cm). I use a tiny skewer to pin the foil together.

4. **Melt** the 2 tablespoons (25 mL) butter in a medium saucepan over low heat and add the flour. Stir and cook for about 2 minutes, without browning.

5. **Add** the hot milk to the mixture, all at once, and stir vigorously with a whisk.

6. **Add** the seasonings. Don't let the sauce get too thick—it should be like a loose custard.

7. **Remove** from the heat to a large bowl and let cool for just a minute or two.

8. **Add** the grated cheddar and Swiss cheeses to the milk mixture. Stir until the cheeses are well combined.

9. **Add** the egg yolks one at a time, whisking well after each addition. Set aside to cool.

10. **Beat** the egg whites to stiff shining peaks.

11. Now comes the only sensitive part. **Ladle** about a quarter of the egg whites into the cheese mixture and blend well. Then pour the cheese mixture into the egg whites. Gently fold until all is well blended. If the phone rings, don't answer it.

12. You can **cover** the mixture with foil at this point and leave it refrigerated no more than 1 hour before baking.

13. **Pour** the mixture into the prepared baking dish.

14. **Set** the dish in a *bain-marie* (a large pan filled with at least 1″ [2.5 cm] of water into which you will put your baking dish). As this water warms, it will help to set the custard in the soufflé.

15. **Bake** in the middle of a preheated oven until the top has browned and the soufflé has risen. This should take about 25 minutes. Test the soufflé with a slightly wet skewer for doneness.

16. **Remove** from the oven, quickly remove the collar, and serve your beautiful creation.

My mother's blintz-making days were ones you wanted to stay out of the kitchen. She might try to get you to help—or worse still, to clean up the mess.

While this recipe is not difficult, it really requires an assembly line. Once you get the rhythm going, you'll be all right. And I promise you that once you make these, you will NEVER eat any other blintzes ever again.

The trick with blintzes is making the crêpes. I often start off with the batter just a bit too thick and then add small amounts of milk till I get it just right. The batter should be the consistency of heavy cream. Another tip—use a blender to mix the batter dough and let the dough rest in the fridge for at least half an hour before starting the crêpes.

Use a small nonstick frying pan or crêpe pan to cook the crêpes. Ever so lightly—I mean barely—butter the pan with paper towel. The temperature of the pan is crucial, much like making pancakes. As a matter of fact, much like making pancakes, the first batch or two is often not quite right. The pan is either too hot or not hot enough. There's too much butter and the batter is too thick. So be prepared to throw away those first few tries until everything is just right.

Use a small soup ladle to pour a bit less than $^1/_2$ a cup (125 mL) of batter into the hot pan. Swirl the batter over the bottom of the pan until it is covered and pour out any excess to ensure that the crêpe is really thin.

Place the pan back on the heat and cook until the top of the crêpe is dry and the edges are slightly browned and coming away from the pan. Adjust the heat if the crêpe isn't cooking just right. The success of your crêpes really depends on your pan and the batter, so trial and error will be your guide. Repaint the pan ever so slightly with butter with every other crêpe or so.

Place each crêpe on a clean dish towel until cool. When I am really going strong, I am able to fill the crêpes and make new ones like a blintz magician.

Grandma Jeanne's Amazing Blintzes

20 crêpes

Batter:

¾ cup	all-purpose flour	175 mL
1 scant cup	milk	250 mL
1 Tbsp	corn oil	15 mL
2	eggs	2
½ tsp	kosher or coarse salt	2 mL

Filling:

½ lb	creamed cottage cheese	250 g
½ lb	dry cottage cheese	250 g
2 Tbsp	fresh lemon juice	25 mL
1	egg	1
	Granulated sugar to taste, about ¼ cup (50 mL)	
½ tsp	kosher or coarse salt	2 mL

For the batter:

1. **Put** all the ingredients into the blender and blend well. Refrigerate for at least 30 minutes to let the batter rest.

For the crêpes:

2. **Brush** a hot, nonstick crêpe pan or 7″ (18 cm) frying pan with a bit of butter. Then remove the excess with a paper towel to ensure that there is just a bit of grease on the pan.

3. **Add** enough batter to cover the surface, tilting the pan to ensure it is all covered. The more the batter, the thicker the crêpe. Crêpes should be thin! You may need to throw away the first few tries. If the batter appears to be too thick, add milk and stir well. The crêpes are done when they start to come away from the sides of the pan.

4. **Cook** on one side only and then turn the crêpes onto a dish towel to cool.

For the filling:

5. While making the crêpes, **combine** all the filling ingredients. Taste to adjust the sugar.

To assemble:

6. The cooked side is the inside of the crêpe. **Fill** each cooled crêpe with about 1 tablespoon (15 mL) of filling and roll up. The crêpes look best just rolled,

but if you want to ensure that they don't come apart when you fry them, close the ends as well. They can be frozen at this point.

To serve:

7. **Sauté** the crêpes in butter in a sauté pan until browned and warmed through.

Serve with sour cream and/or strawberry jam (see Pa's Strawberry Jam, page 253). My mouth is watering!

That's me—the one with the chin—and my big brother, Larry. I was five and he was twelve.

Being quiet, shy, sensitive, and contained, my son Andrew is not easy to get to know. As the middle child in a noisy, assertive family, it must have been hard to be heard. He'd often look at the rest of us like we were all nuts. Often he was quite right.

What saved him is his love of music and his talent for it. Through music, he could, in fact, soar. A proud mother speaks.

Andy is a true romantic with a wonderfully droll sense of humor. He has recently reinvented himself and started a new life, achieving remarkable success.

This is one of his favorite breakfast dishes.

Andy, at thirteen, with me.

Andy's French Toast

Serves 2		
3	eggs	3
½ tsp	kosher or coarse salt	2 mL
½ cup	milk or cream	125 mL
1 Tbsp	maple syrup	15 mL
2 Tbsp	butter	25 mL
4 slices	challah or egg bread	4 slices

1. **Mix** the eggs, salt, milk (or cream), and maple syrup until well blended.

2. **Melt** the butter in a medium sauté pan.

3. **Dip** the bread into the egg mixture one slice at a time and soak for a minute or two until the egg has permeated the bread.

4. **Remove** the bread from the egg mixture, letting the excess run off.

5. **Gently place** the bread into the hot butter and sauté until golden brown. Turn the bread and brown the underside.

Serve with warm maple syrup or Pa's Strawberry Jam (page 253).

Seafood

I remember when I was a young and rather poor single mother; fish was the dish to serve when the cash was running out. I could feed my family for under $2.00. My, oh my, how times have changed. Fish is now popular and consequently expensive. Yet some of my favorite recipes, particularly for entertaining, are for fish.

My mother always taught me not to scrimp on buying food for my table. That being said, I go to the best fishmonger in the city and rely on him to give me fresh, fresh fish. Do the same.

Liz's Striped Bass with Leeks

Serves 6

2 tsp	freshly ground pepper	10 mL
1 tsp	granulated sugar	5 mL
1 tsp	fresh rosemary, finely chopped	5 mL
6	6 oz/170 g striped bass fillets	6

Purée (can be prepared one day in advance):

3	garlic cloves, unpeeled	3
10	whole shallots, unpeeled	10
2 tsp	kosher or coarse salt	10 mL
1 tsp	freshly ground black pepper	5 mL
2 Tbsp	olive oil	25 mL
1/3 cup	heavy (35%) cream	75 mL

Leeks (can be prepared one day in advance):

1 cup	leeks, white part only	250 mL
1 cup	water	250 mL
1/2 cup	granulated sugar	125 mL
2 tsp	lemon rind, grated	10 mL

Vinaigrette (can be prepared one day in advance):

1 cup	extra-virgin olive oil	250 mL
1/2 cup	white wine vinegar	125 mL
4	shallots, finely chopped	4
1 tsp	granulated sugar	5 mL
	Kosher or coarse salt and freshly ground pepper to taste	
1 Tbsp	finely chopped chives	15 mL
1 tsp	butter	5 mL
2 tsp	olive oil	10 mL

Preheat the oven to 375°F (190°C)

1. **Combine** the pepper, sugar, and rosemary.

2. Using a sharp knife, **make** crosses on the skin of each fish fillet. Be careful that you don't penetrate the meat of the fish.

3. **Rub** the spice mixture into both sides of the fish and marinate, covered, for 1 hour.

For the purée:

4. **Put** the garlic and shallots into a baking dish. Sprinkle with the salt, pepper, and olive oil. Cover with aluminum foil and bake in the oven until soft, about 30 minutes. Let cool to room temperature.

5. **Peel** the garlic and shallots and purée in a food processor with the heavy cream. Set aside.

For the leeks:

6. **Cover** a baking sheet with a silpat pad or parchment paper.

7. **Clean** and thinly slice the leeks. (See "Susie's Rules," page 265, for cleaning leeks.)

8. **Combine** the water, sugar, and lemon rind in a medium saucepan. Cook over medium heat until the mixture turns a golden color. Stir the leeks into the caramel mixture and scrape onto the baking sheet. Cool, separating the leeks. Set aside.

For the vinaigrette:

9. **Place** the extra-virgin olive oil, vinegar, shallots, sugar, salt, and pepper in a blender and blend until well combined.

10. **Stir** in the chives and set aside.

To serve:

11. **Melt** the butter and oil in a large nonstick skillet over medium heat. When the pan is hot, add the fish and cook until firm to the touch, about 2 minutes a side.

12. **Place** portions of the shallot and garlic purée in the center of six dinner plates and place the fish over the purée. Sprinkle with the caramelized leeks.

13. **Pour** some of the vinaigrette on each plate in a circle around the fish. Serve immediately.

A superb summer dish because it's best prepared on the barbeque. The corn salsa is what makes this dish so special.

Swordfish and Salsa

Serves 6

Corn salsa:

4	ears fresh corn (If fresh corn is not available, use frozen.)	4
2 Tbsp	ground cumin	25 mL
1 Tbsp	chili powder	15 mL
1/4 cup	fresh oregano, chopped	50 mL
2	garlic cloves, minced	2
2	avocados, peeled and diced	2
1	red bell pepper, seeded and diced	1
1	red or sweet onion, minced	1
14 drops	Tabasco sauce	14 drops
1/2 cup	fresh lime juice	125 mL
1 tsp	kosher or coarse salt	5 mL
1/4 tsp	freshly ground pepper	1 mL
1/4 cup	olive oil	50 mL
1/3 cup	red wine vinegar	75 mL

Fish:

1/4 cup	olive oil	50 mL
1/2 cup	mixed fresh herbs, such as oregano, Italian parsley, thyme, and basil, coarsely chopped	125 mL
3	garlic cloves, minced	3
2 tsp	crushed red pepper	10 mL
1/4 cup	fresh lemon juice	50 mL
	Kosher or coarse salt and freshly ground pepper to taste	
4	swordfish steaks (8 oz/250 g each), 1" (2.5 cm) thick	4

For the salsa:

1. **Remove** the husks and silks from the corn and cut the kernels off the cobs.

2. **Blanch** the corn in boiling water for 3 minutes, drain, and cool in an ice bath.

3. **Mix** the remaining salsa ingredients. Add the corn. Chill until ready to serve. Can be refrigerated, covered, 2 to 3 days. Bring to room temperature before serving.

For the fish:

4. **Combine** the herbs, oil, garlic, red pepper, lemon juice, salt, and pepper in a small mixing bowl. Rub mixture generously over the fish steaks. Marinate the steaks for 1 hour.

5. **Heat** the charcoal grill or broiler.

6. **Grill** the steaks 5 minutes per side. If you want to create grill marks, turn the steaks 90 degrees after cooking for 2 minutes on each side.

Serve immediately topping with room temperature salsa.

Summer of 1948: I am thirteen, at Camp Tioga with Mom and Dad on visitors' day.

Sweet and Sour Whole Fish

Serves 4

2 lbs	whole red snapper	1 kg
½ tsp	kosher or coarse salt	2 mL
¼ tsp	freshly ground pepper	1 mL
4 cups + 2 Tbsp	corn oil	1 L + 25 mL
1	egg yolk, beaten	1
	Potato starch, for dredging	
2	garlic cloves, minced	2
1	small carrot, grated	1
½	red pepper, cored and thinly sliced	½
2	green onions, shredded	2

Sauce:

4 Tbsp	white wine vinegar	50 mL
3 Tbsp	granulated sugar	45 mL
2 Tbsp	ketchup	25 mL
1 Tbsp	sesame oil	15 mL
½ tsp	potato starch	2 mL
¼ tsp	kosher or coarse salt	1 mL
¼ tsp	freshly ground pepper	1 mL
¾ cup	water or chicken stock, homemade preferred	175 mL

1. Using a sharp knife, **make** five crosses on each side of the fish. Be careful that you don't penetrate the meat.

2. **Rub** the fish inside and out with salt and pepper and put aside for 10 minutes.

3. **Prepare** the sauce by combining the vinegar, sugar, ketchup, sesame oil, potato starch, salt, pepper, and stock.

4. **Preheat** 4 cups (1 L) of the oil over high heat in a wok or a deep sauté pan.

5. **Coat** the entire fish with the egg yolk and dredge with the potato starch, shaking off the excess.

6. **Carefully slide** the fish into the wok and deep-fry for about 3 minutes on each side. When the slits open up, the fish is ready to turn over.

7. **Heat** a clean wok and add 2 tablespoons (25 mL) oil.

8. **Add** the garlic and stir until slightly cooked but not brown. Add the carrot and red pepper, and stir-fry for 1 minute.

9. **Add** the sauce and stir until it thickens and the vegetables are evenly coated.

10. **Add** the fish into the mixture, cover the pan, and turn the heat to low, to cook for 1 minute.

11. **Remove** the fish and the sauce to a serving platter. Sprinkle the green onion shreds on top and serve.

Most good things in life are simple, particularly when it comes to food. The really best cooks that I know are able to put a few ingredients together on a whim and create something wonderful. However, all these great meals have relied on superb ingredients. The eggs are fresh, the vegetables are almost "just picked," the meat is perfectly marbled, and the fish is always, always FRESH.

There was a man who used to have a restaurant in town. Simple but good. Poor soul, his life got very complicated because of drugs, and he disappeared. Just before he left I took my children, Owen and Liz, to a cooking class he held. He was so smashed, it was difficult to follow him. We wrote frantically, trying to capture his every word. Here is his simple fish, in a combination of our translations.

Grilled Fish

Serves 2		
1–1½ lbs	whole red snapper or bass	500–750 g
1–2	garlic cloves, thinly sliced	1–2
½ cup	Italian parsley, coarsely chopped	125 mL
	Juice of 1 lemon	
	Kosher or coarse salt and freshly ground pepper to taste	
½ cup	whole basil leaves	125 mL
¼ cup	olive oil	50 mL

1. Using a sharp knife, **make** three or four crosses per side on the skin of the fish. Be careful that you don't penetrate the meat.

2. **Fill** the slashes with the sliced garlic and chopped parsley.

3. **Pour** the lemon juice, salt, and pepper on the fish and in the cavity of the fish.

4. **Fill** the cavity with basil.

5. **Rub** the fish with olive oil.

6. **Grill** or barbeque the fish for 6 minutes per side. Serve with olive oil, balsamic vinegar, lemon juice, and parsley, and accompany with spaghetti and tomato sauce or just a salad.

This is lovely for lunch or with something light, like Grandma Jeanne's Blintzes or a great bowl of soup to start.

Pickled Fish

Serves 6 to 8

4 cups	white vinegar	1 L
4 cups	water	1 L
2 cups	granulated sugar	500 mL
1 Tbsp	kosher or coarse salt	15 mL
3 Tbsp	pickling spice	45 mL
3–4	onions, sliced	3–4
4 lbs	pickerel steaks	2 kg

1. **Bring** all the ingredients, except for the fish, to a boil in a large pot.

2. **Add** the fish and bring to a simmer.

3. **Cook** for about 30 minutes, or until the fish is cooked through.

4. **Remove** the fish to a deep container and pour the strained liquid over it.

5. **Refrigerate.**

Serve cold with hot red horseradish.

My first-born, Liz, is a beautiful girl. I wanted a baby so very badly, but the doctors weren't sure I would be able to have children. Three pregnancies later I found them to be wrong.

Meanwhile, after all the wanting, when she was born I was suddenly terrified. Did not know what to do. How to take care of someone so small who cried all the time. I mean, all the time. I was tempted to change places with her in the crib so that I could get some sleep.

We lived in Virginia Siegel's basement apartment in Pelham (really the Bronx) so that Art, her father, could be close to his work at the hospital where he was a resident training in internal medicine. One big room that was everything for the three of us, save for the toilet—the

Liz as a babe with my mother in Brooklyn.

only place you could go to escape Liz's tears. Somehow I muddled through her first year. Then she finally stopped crying and became a delightful, pudgy little girl.

Liz has grown into a beautiful woman. Bright and talented. Charming and funny. Remarkably competent and organized. A very complex person who doesn't know her own worth. I spend a lot of time wondering what part I had in creating her self-doubts.

I believe I have utterly intimidated her in the kitchen and find only now that she seems to enjoy the creativity of cooking.

Three generations—Mom, me, and Liz on my wedding day in 1981.

Liz's Salmon

Serves 4		
4	salmon steaks	4

Marinade (save to heat for the sauce):

3 Tbsp	sherry	45 mL
3 Tbsp	brown sugar	45 mL
2 Tbsp	water	25 mL
2 Tbsp	soy sauce	25 mL
2 Tbsp	corn oil	25 mL
1½ tsp	minced ginger	7 mL
2 tsp	minced garlic	10 mL

Preheat the broiler

1. **Combine** all of the marinade ingredients.

2. **Marinate** the fish for 1 hour, covered.

3. **Remove** the fish from the marinade and save any leftover sauce.

4. **Set** under the broiler about 6" (15 cm) from the flame and cook for 3 minutes a side, or until opaque in the center.

5. **Heat** the reserved marinade in a saucepan and serve over the cooked fish.

Agreat dish for entertaining. The sauce and the topping can be made ahead. All that remains is baking the fish.

Baked Salmon with Lemon-Thyme Crumb Topping

Serves 6

³/₄ cup	freshly grated Parmigiano-Reggiano cheese	175 mL
¹/₂ cup	chopped Italian parsley	125 mL
¹/₄ cup	chopped fresh thyme or 1 Tbsp (15 mL) crumbled dried thyme	50 mL
2 tsp	grated lemon peel	10 mL
¹/₂ tsp	kosher or coarse salt	2 mL
¹/₄ tsp	freshly ground pepper	1 mL
4	garlic cloves	4
1¹/₂ cups	fresh bread crumbs (see page 247)	345 mL
4 Tbsp	melted butter	50 mL
1	salmon fillet (3¹/₂ lb/1.75 kg)	1
2 Tbsp	soft butter	25 mL

1. **Place** Parmigiano-Reggiano, parsley, thyme, lemon peel, salt, and pepper in a food processor.

2. **Drop** the garlic through the feed tube while the machine is running and process the mixture until it is finely chopped.

3. **Transfer** to a medium-sized bowl.

4. **Add** the bread crumbs and stir to combine. Can be prepared 1 day ahead. Cover and refrigerate. Bring to room temperature before using.

5. When ready to proceed, **toss** the bread crumb mixture with the melted butter.

Preheat the oven to 350°F (180°C)

6. **Generously butter** a shallow baking pan.

7. **Brush** the salmon with 2 tablespoons of soft butter. Cover with the bread crumb mixture, pressing the mixture onto the flesh of the salmon.

8. **Bake** the fish until it's opaque in the center, about 20 minutes.

Serve with Parsley Mayonnaise (page 90).

Parsley Mayonnaise

Makes about 1½ cups (375 mL)		
¼ cup	green onions, minced	50 mL
½ cup	Italian parsley, minced	125 mL
⅓ cup	cilantro, minced	75 mL
1	garlic clove, minced	1
2 Tbsp	red wine vinegar	25 mL
½ tsp	minced fresh oregano or ¼ tsp (1 mL) crumbled dried oregano	2 mL
¼ tsp	kosher or coarse salt	1 mL
¼ tsp	freshly ground pepper	1 mL
¼ tsp	cayenne pepper	1 mL
1 cup	mayonnaise	250 mL

1. **Combine** all the ingredients except the mayonnaise in a small bowl.

2. **Cover** and let stand at room temperature for at least 30 minutes or overnight.

3. **Stir** in the mayonnaise.

Can be prepared 1 day ahead. Cover and refrigerate.

The next recipe comes from Bubbie Wigderson, my first mother-in-law. She was a strong, domineering woman long before it was popular. She had the good sense to appear to be quite docile, but underneath beat the heart of a tiger. Her husband, Poppa, was a dear, sweet, gentle man. I doubt if he would have survived without her.

She led the family upward, determined that they would all succeed. When her son, Arthur, was born, she decided at his birth that he would grow up to be a doctor. Choosing this profession for one's son meant choosing success. This choice was natural for many European Jewish immigrants. After all, you couldn't get a job in the banks, the insurance industry, or any large corporations. You would have to have your own business or be a professional (your own business) to survive the anti-Semitism that existed at that time in Canada. So being a son meant having a profession. That being a doctor was not his choice, or even a good choice for the son, made no difference.

Bubbie was not a great cook. Frankly, I don't think it interested her. I knew she wasn't a great cook before I met her: her son ordered his meat well done. This is a dead giveaway—Mother must have overcooked it.

However, her salmon patties are good. An easy meal. Accompany with some sliced beefsteak tomatoes.

Bubbie's Salmon Patties

Serves 4

2	tins (each 6 oz/ 170 g) good-quality salmon, skin and bones removed	2
1	onion, grated	1
1	carrot, grated	1
1/3 cup	corn flake crumbs	75 mL
4	eggs, beaten	4
1 tsp	Italian parsley, finely chopped	5 mL
1 tsp	Worcestershire sauce	5 mL
1 splash	Tabasco sauce	1 splash
	Kosher or coarse salt and freshly ground pepper to taste	
	Corn oil	

1. **Drain** the salmon and remove the skin and bones.
2. **Mix** the salmon with all the ingredients except the oil.
3. **Form** the mixture with the palms of your hands into small patties, about 2" (5 cm) in diameter.
4. **Heat** the oil in a heated sauté pan and cook the patties until lightly browned.
5. **Place** the patties on paper towels to drain.

Serve warm.

This dish is so rich and pure that I serve it with a lightly tossed salad, c'est tout!

Steamed Lobster

Serves 2

	Bouquet garni (see "Susie's Rules," page 262)	
3 Tbsp	peppercorns	45 mL
3 Tbsp	kosher or coarse salt	45 mL
½ cup	fresh lemon juice	125 mL
1 cup	white wine	250 mL
2	lobsters (female preferred, 1 lb/ 500 g)	2
2	lemons, halved	2
½ cup	melted butter	125 mL

1. **Bring** a very large stockpot filled two-thirds with cold water to a boil.

2. **Add** the bouquet garni, peppercorns, salt, lemon juice, and white wine. Simmer for 5 minutes.

3. **Add** the lobsters to the boiling bouillon, cover, and boil until done, about 10 to 12 minutes. The shell should be red.

4. **Break** the lobster into pieces as follows:
   - Split the lobster down its back.
   - Remove the small sac behind the head.
   - Separate the claws from the body, wrap them with a dishcloth, and use a hammer to crack the claws.
   - Separate the tail from the body.

Serve with sliced lemon and melted butter—and lots of napkins.

Mom and Dad on their wedding day.

My mother and father were both brought up on the Lower East Side of New York. This was where the Italian, Russian, Polish, Irish, and German immigrants started their lives in their new country, America. Crowded, noisy, and alive with hope, the tenements of the Lower East Side were home to many courageous, honest, and hard-working people.

My mother would describe racing home from school on Fridays to hand wash each piece of the crystal chandelier that hung in the dining room of her tenement apartment. The chandelier was a necessity for my grandfather. Grandfather, he of the big temper, loved beautiful things. His taste was refined, but his pocketbook small. This was because he didn't work. He would dress in his finest, every day. Spats and a cane. Walk the streets of the East Side making friends. Sometime finding work, which he gave my grandmother to do. She was, after all, only a peasant.

The only money he ever made was when he gambled on the numbers. When Uncle Morris, his son, married a "poor girl," Grandfather decided to make the wedding. Of course, there was no money for such an affair. The day before the wedding Grandpa won on a number and was able to pay the bill. This story gave me my first definition of chutzpah.

My mother's wedding was huge and elaborate with caged white doves released at the end of the evening. The affair cost $2,000 in the 1920s. I can't even guess what that would be today. This from the same man who wasn't working.

My grandfather's love of life, his taste, his style, and his desire to have fun were all passed down to his daughter. She was lively and bright, and my father adored and wanted her till the very end. I believe he wisely saw that she would be the woman who would take him out of his shell. That she would see to him, to his home, and to his children.

When my parents were courting they would go to a neighborhood Italian restaurant in Little Italy. Down a flight of narrow stairs to a room crowded with diners. So crowded that new friends were made and food was shared table to table. One of my favorites there was the Lobster Fra Diavolo. Also try my versions of their Mozzarella in Carrozza (page 4) and Fried Zucchini (page 192).

Lobster Fra Diavolo

Serves 2		
2	lobsters (2 lbs/1kg)	2
¼ cup	olive oil	50 mL
2	garlic cloves, minced	2
1	can (28 oz/796 mL) Italian plum tomatoes	1
1 Tbsp	chopped Italian parsley	15 mL
¼ tsp	dried oregano	1 mL
½ tsp	chopped fresh basil	2 mL
	Kosher or coarse salt and freshly ground pepper to taste	
½ tsp	crushed red pepper flakes	2 mL

1. **Break** the lobster into pieces as follows:
   - Split the lobster down its back.
   - Remove the small sac behind the head.
   - Separate the claws from the body.
   - Wrap the claws with a dishcloth and use a hammer to crack the claws.
   - Separate the tail from the body.

2. **Heat** the olive oil in a heavy sauté pan. When the oil is hot, add the lobster, meat side down. Simmer for 10 minutes. Turn the lobster.

3. **Add** the garlic, tomatoes, parsley, oregano, basil, salt, pepper, and pepper flakes and cook slowly for 15 minutes.

Serve very hot. Or you can cook some spaghetti and toss with the Fra Diavolo. Soaks up the sauce. Remember to have a bone dish available.

Suzanne's Quick and Easy Shrimp

Serves 2		
½ lb	shrimp	250 g
2 Tbsp	olive oil	25 mL
2 Tbsp	finely minced garlic	25 mL
½ cup	white wine	125 mL
½ cup	chicken stock, homemade preferred	125 mL
1	bay leaf	1
1 Tbsp	butter	15 mL
	Kosher or coarse salt and freshly ground pepper	
⅓ cup	chopped Italian parsley	75 mL

1. **Clean** the shrimp. (See "Susie's Rules," page 267, for directions on peeling and deveining shrimp.)
2. **Add** the olive oil to a heated sauté pan.
3. **Add** the shrimp and quickly stir-fry only until they become pink.
4. **Add** the garlic and cook for a moment, ensuring that the garlic does not burn.
5. **Add** the white wine, stock, and bay leaf, cooking for 1 minute.
6. **Remove** the shrimp to a plate.
7. **Reduce** the liquid to about half and add the butter to thicken the sauce.
8. **Season** with salt and pepper.
9. **Add** the shrimp and parsley to the pan to heat with the sauce. Remove the bay leaf.

Serve at once.

I *do* like garlic. A lot.

Baked Lemon Shrimp with Garlic

Serves 6

2 lbs	large shrimp (about 30)	1 kg
½ cup	butter	125 mL
2 Tbsp	minced garlic, or to taste	25 mL
½ cup	chopped Italian parsley	125 mL
½ tsp	kosher or coarse salt	2 mL
Dash	freshly ground pepper	Dash
2 Tbsp	freshly grated lemon zest, from about 2 large lemons	25 mL
	Juice of 2 large lemons	

Preheat the oven to 450°F (230°C)

1. **Clean** the shrimp. (See "Susie's Rules," page 267, for directions on peeling and deveining shrimp.)
2. **Melt** the butter with salt over moderately low heat.
3. **Stir** in the garlic and half the parsley.
4. **Add** the shrimp and season with salt and pepper.
5. **Bake** the shrimp for 5 minutes in a large baking dish where the shrimp will fit in one layer.
6. **Turn** the shrimp and sprinkle with the remaining parsley, zest, and lemon juice.
7. **Bake** the shrimp until just cooked through, 5 to 10 minutes more.
8. **Brown** for a moment under broiler.

Serve the shrimp with lemon wedges and lots of bread for dunkin'.

Sautéed Scallops with Fried Spinach

Serves 6

24	sea scallops, halved crosswise	24
	Milk	
	Kosher or coarse salt and freshly ground pepper to taste	
2	plum tomatoes	2
40	small garlic cloves, peeled	40
	Corn oil	
1 cup	fish stock or bottled clam juice	250 mL
1 cup	butter, at room temperature	250 mL
1 bunch	spinach, washed, dried, stemmed, and cut into julienne strips	1 bunch
	All-purpose flour	
2 Tbsp	butter	25 mL

1. **Place** scallops in a medium bowl. Add enough milk to cover.

2. **Season** with salt and freshly ground pepper. Refrigerate for at least 2 hours.

3. **Peel,** seed, and chop the tomatoes. (See "Susie's Rules," page 267, for peeling tomatoes.) Set aside.

4. **Blanch** the garlic in a saucepan of boiling water for 2 minutes. Drain, rinse, and repeat the blanching process.

5. **Add** 1 tablespoon (15 mL) corn oil and the garlic to a heavy skillet. By adding the garlic to room-temperature oil, you prevent the garlic from burning.

6. **Sauté** over medium heat until golden brown, about 5 minutes.

7. **Transfer** 10 of the garlic cloves to a heavy medium saucepan, reserving the remaining 30 cloves for later use.

8. **Add** the fish stock to the saucepan and boil until reduced by half, about 5 minutes. (This can be prepared 1 day ahead. Cover the stock mixture and the remaining thirty garlic cloves in separate containers and refrigerate. Once you remove the stock mixture from the refrigerator, bring it to a boil before proceeding.)

9. **Transfer** the stock mixture to a blender, add the 1 cup (250 mL) of butter, and mix until smooth.

10. Meanwhile, **heat** more of the oil in a deep fryer or heavy large saucepan to 375° F (190° C).

11. **Add** the spinach and fry until crisp, about 3 minutes. Be very careful as the oil tends to spatter.

12. **Drain** the spinach and season with salt.

13. **Remove** the scallops from the refrigerator, drain, and pat dry. Dredge in flour.

14. **Melt** the 2 tablespoons (25 mL) of butter with 2 tablespoons (25 mL) of corn oil in a large skillet over high heat.

15. **Add** the scallops and sauté until golden brown, turning occasionally, about 3 minutes.

16. **Mound** the spinach in the center of each plate and surround with 8 scallop halves.

17. **Spoon** the sauce around the outer edge of the plate. Set 5 garlic cloves in the sauce. Garnish with tomato.

Serve immediately.

Pastas and Rice

I love to eat all food, but I love to *cook* Italian food most of all. I think it's because you can feel it as you do it. Seasoning is the chef's choice and so your mood and personality affect your creations.

I always cook my pasta al dente and, you will note, I almost always add 1 tablespoon (15 mL) of butter to the sauced pasta just before serving.

When making any of the tomato sauces, add a whole, unpeeled potato about 20 minutes before completion. Nicely thickens the sauce.

I've also included three recipes for rice dishes in this section.

Owen's Carbonara Sauce

Serves 2

1 Tbsp	olive oil	15 mL
¼ lb	pancetta, cut into 1" (2.5 cm) cubes (This Italian bacon can be found in most markets. Use any other bacon if you can't find it.)	125 g
1	bay leaf, crumbled	1
1	small onion, diced	1
½ tsp	dried oregano	2 mL
⅛ tsp	red pepper flakes	0.5 mL
	Kosher or coarse salt (careful, the pancetta is quite salty) and freshly ground pepper to taste	
½ cup	white wine	125 mL
2	egg yolks, at room temperature	2
½ cup	heavy (35%) cream, or more, to thicken	125 mL
⅔ cup	grated Parmigiano-Reggiano cheese	150 mL
4 Tbsp	kosher or coarse salt	250 mL
½ lb	penne	250 g

1. **Add** the olive oil to a heated sauté pan.

2. **Brown** the pancetta in the pan with the bay leaf.

3. **Remove** the pancetta from the pan and put aside.

4. **Add** the onions to the fat and cook till golden.

5. **Add** the pancetta to the onions, along with the oregano, pepper flakes, salt, and pepper.

6. **Add** the white wine to reduce. Remove the bay leaf.

7. **Whisk** the egg yolks, cream, and cheese in a small bowl and set aside.

8. **Bring** 8 quarts (8 L) water to boil in a large pot and add the salt. The water should taste like the sea.

9. **Add** the penne and stir frequently with a wooden fork. Follow the instructions on the package, but make sure that you taste for al dente. This should take at least 15 minutes.

10. **Drain** the pasta and toss with the onion and pancetta mixture over medium heat.

11. **Remove** from the heat, add the egg mixture, and stir. Taste for seasoning.

Penne with Spinach and Ricotta Cheese

Serves 4 to 6

1 lb	young spinach, washed and dried well	500 g
2 Tbsp	olive oil	25 mL
1 Tbsp	chopped shallots	15 mL
	Kosher or coarse salt and freshly ground pepper to taste	
1 cup	ricotta cheese	250 mL
1 cup	half-and-half (10%) cream	250 mL
Pinch	ground nutmeg	Pinch
2 Tbsp	butter	25 mL
3 Tbsp	kosher or coarse salt	45 mL
1 lb	penne	500 g
½ cup	freshly grated Parmigiano-Reggiano cheese	125 mL
1 Tbsp	butter	15 mL

1. **Chiffonade** the spinach. (See the directions for chiffonade in "Susie's Rules," page 264).

2. **Heat** the olive oil in a large heated sauté pan.

3. **Add** the shallots and cook until they are softened, about 5 minutes.

4. **Stir** in the spinach, a pinch of salt, and the pepper. Cover and steam the spinach until it wilts, about 5 minutes.

5. Meanwhile, in a small bowl, **stir** together the ricotta, cream, and nutmeg until smooth.

6. **Stir** the ricotta mixture and the butter into the spinach and season with salt and pepper. Reduce the heat to medium low and simmer for 2 to 3 minutes.

7. **Bring** 8 quarts (8 L) water to a boil in a large pot and add 3 tablespoons (45 mL) of salt. The water should taste like the sea. Add the penne and stir frequently with a wooden fork. Follow the instructions on the package, but make sure that you taste for al dente. This should take about 15 minutes.

8. **Reserve** ¹/₂ cup (125 mL) of the pasta cooking liquid. Drain the pasta well and return it to the pot over low heat.

9. **Add** the spinach mixture and enough of the reserved cooking liquid to make a sauce that lightly coats the pasta. Toss thoroughly.

10. **Remove** the pot from the heat and stir in the grated cheese and 1 tablespoon (15 mL) of butter.

Age fourteen—the dress was navy-blue organdy. Now why would I remember that?

Penne with Cauliflower and Pecorino

Serves 4

4 Tbsp	olive oil	50 mL
1	large onion, diced	1
2	garlic cloves, minced	2
2	shallots, chopped	2
3	anchovy fillets	3
1 tsp	red pepper flakes	5 mL
1 head	cauliflower	1 head
3 Tbsp	kosher or coarse salt	45 mL
1 lb	penne	500 g
½ cup	grated pecorino Romano or Parmigiano-Reggiano cheese	125 ml
½ cup	chopped Italian parsley	125 mL
2 Tbsp	butter	25 mL
	Kosher or coarse salt and freshly ground pepper to taste	

1. **Heat** the olive oil in a large hot sauté pan until hot, add the onion, and cook until it is translucent.
2. **Add** the garlic and shallots, stirring well and ensuring that the garlic does not brown.
3. **Add** the anchovies and red pepper flakes. Cook until the anchovies melt, about 5 minutes.
4. **Core** the cauliflower and remove the leaves and base. Slice the leaves and cut the florets into bite-size pieces.
5. **Put** all the cauliflower into the sauté pan with the onion mixture. Lower the heat to medium-low and cook, stirring regularly, for about 7 to 10 minutes, until the cauliflower is softened and light brown but not mushy.
6. **Bring** 8 quarts (8 L) water to boil in a large pot and add the salt. The water should taste like the sea. Add the penne and stir frequently with a wooden fork. Follow the instructions on the package, but make sure that you taste for al dente. This should take at least 15 minutes.
7. After the penne is cooked, **drain,** saving some of the pasta water.
8. **Toss** the hot pasta into the pan with the cauliflower. You may want to add ½ cup (125 mL) of the pasta water.
9. **Add** the grated cheese, salt, pepper, parsley and butter. Toss to coat and serve immediately.

The peas should be fresh, just off the vine. If this is not possible, use frozen peas.

Penne and Peas

Serves 4

3 Tbsp	kosher or coarse salt	45 mL
1 lb	penne	500 g
1/4 cup	olive oil	50 mL
1/2	sweet white or red onion, diced	1/2
2	small garlic cloves, minced	2
3 oz	prosciutto ham, cut into medium dice	75 g
1 cup	white wine	250 mL
3 cups	fresh or frozen peas	750 mL
	Kosher or coarse salt and freshly ground pepper to taste	
1 Tbsp	butter	15 mL
	Grated Parmigiano-Reggiano cheese, to taste	

1. **Bring** 8 quarts (8 L) water to boil in a large pot and add the salt. The water should taste like the sea. Add the penne and stir frequently with a wooden fork. Follow the instructions on the package, but make sure that you taste for al dente. This should take about 15 minutes.

2. **Drain** the penne, reserving 1 cup (250 mL) of the pasta water.

3. **Heat** the olive oil in a hot sauté pan while the penne is cooking. Add the onion and garlic and cook until translucent. Check frequently to ensure that the garlic does not burn.

4. **Add** the prosciutto to heat through.

5. **Add** the white wine and cook on high heat till it reduces by about half.

6. **Add** the peas and cook for 2 minutes, just till they are al dente.

7. **Season** with salt and pepper.

8. **Toss** the peas and penne. If the sauce is too dry, add some of the reserved pasta water.

9. **Add** the butter and cheese and serve immediately.

Penne with Sausage and Red Pepper

Serves 4		
1 Tbsp	olive oil	15 mL
4	sweet Italian sausages	4
1	onion, diced	1
1	shallot, diced	1
1	garlic clove, minced	1
2	red peppers, sliced thinly	2
¼ tsp	red pepper flakes	1 mL
	Kosher or coarse salt and freshly ground pepper to taste	
3 Tbsp	kosher or coarse salt	45 mL
1 lb	penne	500 g
1 Tbsp	butter	15 mL
4 Tbsp	parsley, chopped	50 mL

1. **Heat** the oil in a large heated skillet.

2. **Slice** the sausage down the middle, remove the skin, and break the meat up into the pan.

3. **Cook** until browned. Remove the meat from the pan and set aside, leaving behind the oil and fat.

4. **Add** the onion, shallot, and minced garlic to the pan. Lightly sauté until translucent, making sure the garlic does not burn.

5. **Add** the red peppers. When they have softened slightly, add the meat, pepper flakes, salt, and pepper. The sauce can be made 1 day in advance.

6. **Bring** 8 quarts (8 mL) water to a boil in a large pot and add 3 tablespoons (45 mL) of salt. The water should taste like the sea. Add the penne and stir frequently with a wooden fork. Follow the instructions on the package, but make sure that you taste for al dente. This should take about 15 minutes.

7. **Reserve** 1/2 cup (125 mL) of the pasta cooking water and drain the penne.

8. **Toss** the penne with the sauce. Add the reserved water as required and the butter. Sprinkle with parsley.

Spaghetti with White Clam Sauce

4 servings

½ cup	olive oil	125 mL
3	large garlic cloves, minced	3
1	large shallot, chopped	1
½ tsp	red pepper flakes	2 mL
2 lbs	Manila clams, soaked in cold water for 2 hours and scrubbed	1 kg
1	bay leaf	1
½ cup	dry white wine	125 mL
1 cup	bottled clam juice	250 mL
5 Tbsp	chopped Italian parsley	75 mL
1 Tbsp	butter	15 mL
3 Tbsp	kosher or coarse salt	45 mL
1 lb	spaghetti	500 g
	Kosher or coarse salt and freshly ground pepper to taste	
1 Tbsp	butter	15 mL

1. **Combine** the olive oil, garlic, shallot, and pepper flakes in a large, cold, deep sauté pan and cook over moderate heat until the garlic is almost golden, about 5 minutes.

2. **Add** the clams and the bay leaf, cover, and cook over high heat, stirring occasionally, until the clams open, 5 to 8 minutes.

3. **Check** the pan often to remove the open clams. With a slotted spoon, transfer the clams to a bowl and set aside. Throw away any clams that do not open.

4. **Quickly add** the wine to the pan and cook over high heat until reduced to 3 tablespoons (45 mL), about 5 minutes. Remove the bay leaf.

5. **Add** the clam juice, parsley, and butter.

6. **Bring** 8 quarts (8 L) water to boil in a large pot and add the salt. The water should taste like the sea. Add the spaghetti and stir frequently with a wooden fork. Follow the instructions on the package, but make sure that you taste for al dente. This should take about 10 minutes.

7. After the spaghetti is cooked, **drain,** saving some of the pasta water.

8. **Add** the spaghetti to the sauce, tossing until most of the broth has been absorbed. If the sauce is too dry, add some of the pasta water.

9. **Add** the butter, season with salt and pepper, and top with the clams.

Andy's Pasta with Divine Tomato Sauce

Serves 4

Freeze ¹/₂ of the tomato sauce base—the remaining ¹/₂ will serve 4

Tomato sauce base:

1	medium leek, both white and green parts	1
¹/₄ cup	olive oil	50 mL
28 oz	canned Italian plum tomatoes	796 mL
1 tsp	granulated sugar	5 mL
1 tsp	kosher or coarse salt	5 mL
¹/₂ tsp	freshly ground pepper	2 mL

Completed sauce:

¹/₂ cup	dried porcini	125 mL
³/₄ cup	hot chicken broth (homemade preferred) or hot water	175 mL
1 Tbsp	olive oil	15 mL
1 Tbsp	sun-dried tomato oil (the oil that sun-dried tomatoes are stored in) or oven-dried tomato oil (see page 249)	15 mL
1 Tbsp	butter	15 mL
3 Tbsp	shallots, chopped	45 mL
1 Tbsp	garlic, minced	15 mL
2 Tbsp	diced sun-dried tomatoes	25 mL
1 tsp	kosher or coarse salt	5 mL
¹/₂ tsp	freshly ground pepper	2 mL
1 Tbsp	Italian parsley, chopped	15 mL
¹/₄ cup	sour cream	50 mL
2 lbs	linguini or spaghetti	1 kg
3 Tbsp	kosher or coarse salt	45 mL
2 Tbsp	butter	25 mL
³/₄ cup	grated Parmigiano-Reggiano cheese	175 mL

1. **Clean** the leeks. (See Susie's Rules," page 265, for cleaning leeks.)
2. **Heat** the olive oil in a large heated skillet.
3. **Dice** the cleaned leek and sauté over medium heat until the leek becomes limp.
4. **Add** the tomatoes with their juice, crushing the tomatoes in your hands over the skillet. Careful, they can explode.
5. Then **add** the sugar, salt, and pepper.

6. **Stir** well to combine and simmer uncovered for 20 minutes or until the sauce has reduced by half. This should yield about 3 cups (750 mL). Once cooled, the sauce can be refrigerated for 1 week or frozen for up to 6 months.

7. **Set** aside half the sauce for this recipe.

8. **Soak** the porcini in the hot broth or water for about 15 minutes.

9. **Drain** the soaked porcini, straining and reserving the liquid for later use. Rinse to remove any remaining grit, squeeze until dry, chop, and set aside. Don't overwash as you will remove much of the great flavor. Just a quick rinse.

10. **Bring** the olive oil to a low heat in a large skillet. Add the sun-dried tomato oil, butter, shallots, and garlic and cook until the shallots become translucent.

11. **Add** 1 1/2 cups (375 mL) of the prepared tomato sauce. Bring the sauce to a simmer.

12. **Add** the porcini and the strained porcini liquid. Simmer the sauce until it is quite thick, about 10 minutes.

13. **Add** the sun-dried tomatoes, 1 teaspoon (5 mL) salt, and pepper. Simmer for 5 minutes over a very low heat.

14. **Add** the parsley and sour cream. Simmer for 1 more minute.

The recipe can be prepared ahead through this step and refrigerated for up to 5 days.

15. When ready to serve, **bring** the sauce to a simmer.

16. **Bring** 8 quarts (8 L) water to a boil in a large pot and add 3 tablespoons (45 mL) of salt. The water should taste like the sea. Add the linguini and

(continues on page 110)

stir frequently with a wooden fork. Follow the instructions on the pack-age, but make sure that you taste for al dente. This should take about 10 minutes.

17. Add the drained pasta to the simmering sauce.

18. Add the butter and cheese and serve at once.

Mother (on the left) and me, both at age sixteen.

Spaghetti with Eggplant

Serves 2

1	medium eggplant, washed	1
	Kosher or coarse salt	
¼ cup	olive oil	50 mL
1	large shallot, diced	1
2	garlic cloves, minced	2
½ tsp	red pepper flakes	2 mL
3 Tbsp	chopped Italian parsley	45 mL
	Kosher or coarse salt and freshly ground pepper to taste	
½ lb	spaghetti	250 g
3 Tbsp	kosher or coarse salt	45 mL
1 Tbsp	butter	15 mL

1. **Cube** the washed eggplant and place on a rack or in a colander. Salt well and allow to drain for 1 hour.

2. **Rinse** the eggplant thoroughly and dry. Remember that it will retain some of the salt if you aren't careful.

3. **Add** the olive oil to a large sauté pan and lightly sauté the shallots and garlic, being careful not to burn the garlic.

4. **Add** the red pepper flakes and the eggplant cubes and sauté until they are lightly brown and caramelized.

5. **Add** the parsley and season with salt and pepper to taste.

6. **Bring** 8 quarts (8 L) water to boil in a large pot and add the 3 tablespoons (45 mL) of salt. The water should taste like the sea. Add the spaghetti and stir frequently with a wooden fork. Follow the instructions on the package, but make sure that you taste for al dente. This should take about 10 minutes.

7. After the spaghetti is cooked, **drain,** saving some of the pasta water.

8. **Toss** the pasta with the eggplant mixture. If it is too dry, add some of the pasta water.

9. **Mix** in the butter and serve immediately.

Spaghetti with Parsnips and Pancetta

Serves 4

3 Tbsp	olive oil	45 mL
1/4 lb	chopped pancetta (This Italian bacon can be found in most markets. Use any other bacon if you can't find it.)	125 g
3 Tbsp	butter	45 mL
1	garlic clove, minced	1
1/2 tsp	red pepper flakes	2 mL
2 lbs	parsnips, peeled, quartered lengthwise, cored, then diced	1 kg
	Kosher or coarse salt and freshly ground pepper to taste	
3 Tbsp	kosher or coarse salt	45 mL
1 lb	spaghetti	500 g
1/2 cup	Italian parsley, chopped	125 mL
1 Tbsp	butter	15 mL
	Grated Parmigiano-Reggiano cheese	

1. **Heat** the oil in a heavy heated skillet. Add the pancetta to sauté over a moderately high heat, stirring frequently, until browned, about 8 minutes. Remove with a slotted spoon and set aside.

2. **Reduce** the heat, add the butter to any fat remaining in the skillet, and then add the garlic and red pepper flakes, cooking quickly so that the garlic does not burn.

3. **Add** the parsnips, salt, and pepper and cook, stirring occasionally, until lightly browned and caramelized, about 15 minutes. Remove from the heat and set aside.

4. **Bring** 8 quarts (8 L) water to a boil in a large pot and add the salt. The water should taste like the sea. Add the spaghetti and stir frequently with a wooden fork. Follow the instructions on the package, but make sure that you taste for al dente. This should take about 10 minutes.

5. **Reserve** 2 cups (500 mL) of the pasta cooking water, and then drain the pasta.

6. **Add** the pasta and 1/2 cup (125 mL) of the reserved cooking water to the parsnips.

7. **Stir in** the pancetta and parsley and toss over moderately high heat for 1 minute. Add more pasta cooking water if necessary. Toss with the chopped parsley and butter.

Serve with grated Parmigiano-Reggiano cheese.

This recipe is simply simple and oh, so delicious. The perciatelli takes a bit of time to properly cook. Check that the pasta is al dente before removing it from the water. I take off a cup of cooking water before draining.

Perciatelli, Pepper, and Cheese

Serves 4

3 Tbsp	kosher or coarse salt	45 mL
1 lb	perciatelli, broken in half	500 g
6 Tbsp	olive oil	90 mL
1 Tbsp	butter	15 mL
1 Tbsp	coarsely ground black pepper	15 mL
1 Tbsp	coarsely ground white pepper	15 mL
1³/₄ cups	freshly grated pecorino Romano cheese (6 oz/170 g)	425 mL
	Kosher or coarse salt to taste	

1. **Bring** 8 quarts (8 L) water to a boil in a large pot and add the 3 tablespoons (45 mL) of salt. The water should taste like the sea. Add the perciatelli and stir frequently with a wooden fork. Follow the instructions on the package, but make sure that you taste for al dente. This should take about 15 to 18 minutes.

2. **Reserve** ¹/₂ cup (125 mL) of the cooking water, then drain the perciatelli and return it to the pot.

3. **Add** the olive oil, butter, black and white pepper, and the reserved pasta water.

4. **Add** half of the cheese.

5. **Season** with salt and toss well.

6. **Transfer** to a large bowl, sprinkle with the remaining cheese, and serve at once.

Pasta with Porcini Mushrooms

Serves 4		
³/₄ oz	dried porcini mushrooms	20 g
³/₄ cup	hot chicken broth, homemade preferred, or hot water	175 mL
1 lb	mix of fresh wild mushrooms and some cultivated mushrooms as well	500 g
¼ cup	olive oil	50 mL
1	large shallot, chopped	1
1	garlic clove, minced	1
½ Tbsp	red pepper flakes	8 mL
½ cup	Italian parsley, chopped	125 mL
1½ cups	heavy (35%) cream	375 mL
3 Tbsp	kosher or coarse salt	45 mL
1 lb	spaghetti or tagliatelle pasta	500 g
	Kosher or coarse salt and freshly ground pepper to taste	
1 Tbsp	butter	15 mL
	Grated Parmigiano-Reggiano cheese	

1. **Soak** the dried porcini mushrooms in the hot broth or hot water for 15 minutes.

2. **Trim** and wipe the fresh mushrooms. Chop coarsely and set aside.

3. **Drain** the soaked porcini, straining and reserving the liquid for later use. Rinse the porcini to remove any remaining grit and squeeze them until dry, chop, and set aside. Don't overwash them as you will remove much of the great flavor—just a quick rinse.

4. **Add** the olive oil to a large skillet and sauté the shallot and garlic for 3 minutes, stirring occasionally and watching that the garlic does not burn.

5. **Add** the red pepper flakes and stir well into shallot mixture.

6. **Increase** the heat, add the parsley, and sauté.

7. **Add** the fresh, chopped mushrooms and sauté for about 15 minutes, or until lightly browned, stirring occasionally.

8. **Add** the dried porcini and cook for 10 more minutes, stirring to incorporate with the fresh mushrooms.

9. **Add** the strained porcini juice. You can prepare the mixture up to this point the day before.

10. When ready to serve, **add** the cream, boiling the sauce to reduce it slightly.

11. **Bring** 8 quarts (8 L) water to boil in a large pot and add the 3 tablespoons (45 mL) of salt. The water should taste like the sea. Add the pasta and stir frequently with a wooden fork. Follow the instructions on the package, but make sure that you taste for al dente.

12. **Drain** the pasta and toss with the sauce. Season with salt and pepper, add butter, and serve immediately.

Serve with grated Parmigiano-Reggiano cheese.

Cheerleading squad at Midwood High School, 1951. I'm on the far right, middle row.

Trudy's Sweet Noodle Pudding

Serves 8

3	eggs, at room temperature	3
1/3 cup	granulated sugar	75 mL
1/2 cup	melted butter, cooled	125 mL
1 cup	cottage cheese	250 mL
3 Tbsp	sour cream	45 mL
1	can (15.5 oz/450 mL) crushed pineapple, drained	1
3 Tbsp	kosher or coarse salt	45 mL
1/2 lb	wide egg noodles	250 g
1 cup	frosted flakes	250 mL
1/4 cup	melted butter	50 mL

Preheat the oven to 350°F (180°C)

1. **Lightly** grease a 10″ × 10″ (25 cm × 25 cm) casserole, preferably one that you can bring to the table.

2. **Separate** the eggs, set aside the egg whites, and beat the yolks with the sugar until creamy.

3. **Add** the cooled butter, cottage cheese, sour cream, and pineapple to the egg yolk and sugar mixture. Combine well.

4. **Bring** 6 quarts (6 L) water to boil in a large pot and add the salt. The water should taste like the sea. Add the noodles and stir frequently with a wooden fork. Follow instructions on the package, but make sure that you taste for al dente. This should take about 7 to 10 minutes. Drain the noodles. Don't cook them too early, as they will stick together like glue. If you forget this word of advice, lightly—and I mean *lightly*—toss the noodles with a bit of butter to keep them separated.

5. **Beat** the egg whites until they are stiff but not dry.

6. **Gently fold** the egg yolk mixture into the beaten egg whites and then add to the cooked noodles.

7. **Pour** this mixture into the casserole dish.

8. **Combine** the frosted flakes with the 1/4 cup (50 mL) of melted butter and pour the mixture over the batter.

9. **Bake** for 40 minutes and serve hot.

An easy, warm, and comforting dish.

Grandma Jeanne's Macaroni Casserole

Serves 4

3 Tbsp	kosher or coarse salt	45 mL
¾ lb	elbow macaroni	375 g
3 Tbsp	vegetable oil	45 mL
1 lb	ground beef	500 g
2	cans (each 10 oz/ 284 mL) tomato soup	2
	Kosher or coarse salt and freshly ground pepper to taste	
¼ tsp	paprika	1 mL
2	onions, diced	2
2	green peppers, diced	2
¾ lb	white mushrooms, sliced	375 g

Preheat the oven to 375°F (190°C)

1. **Bring** 8 quarts (8 L) water to a boil in a large pot and add the 3 tablespoons (45 mL) of salt. The water should taste like the sea. Add the macaroni and stir frequently with a wooden fork. Follow instructions on the package, but make sure that you taste for al dente. This should take about 12 to 14 minutes. Drain and set aside. Don't cook the noodles too early, as they will stick together like glue.

While the macaroni is cooking, prepare the sauce:

2. **Add** 1 tablespoon (15 mL) of the oil to a heated sauté pan. When it is hot, sauté the meat to remove all traces of red, breaking it up with a fork as you cook. Remove the meat from the pan with a slotted spoon and set aside.

3. **Add** the tomato soup, salt, pepper, and paprika to the meat mixture.

4. **Add** the remaining oil to a hot sauté pan and then add the onions, cooking them until they are translucent.

5. **Add** the green peppers and cook till they are limp.

(continues on page 118)

117

6. **Add** the mushrooms and cook them till they are heated through.

7. **Add** the meat mixture to the vegetables and simmer for 5 minutes.

8. **Combine** the meat and vegetable mixture with the cooked macaroni.

9. **Place** in a well-greased casserole and bake for 35 minutes.

Jeanne and George, Mom and Dad, in the early 1970s.

There's nothing simpler or sweeter than sauce made from summer tomatoes with garden-fresh herbs.

Simple Summer Tomato Sauce

Serves 2		
1½ lbs	fresh tomatoes, Italian plum tomatoes preferred	750 g
2 Tbsp	olive oil	25 mL
1	large shallot, finely chopped	1
1	small garlic clove, minced	1
½ cup	white wine	125 mL
1	potato, unpeeled (optional)	1
	Kosher or coarse salt and freshly ground pepper to taste	
⅓ cup	fresh basil	75 mL
1 Tbsp	fresh thyme	15 mL
3 Tbsp	kosher or coarse salt	45 mL
½ lb	spaghetti	250 g
1 Tbsp	butter	15 mL
	Grated Parmigiano-Reggiano cheese, to taste	

1. **Peel,** seed, and chop the tomatoes. (See "Susie's Rules," page 267 for peeling tomatoes.)

2. **Heat** the olive oil in a saucepan over medium-high heat. Add the shallot and garlic, cooking until the shallot is translucent. Watch carefully to ensure that the garlic does not burn.

3. **Add** the fresh tomatoes and stir.

4. **Raise** the heat and add the white wine. If you want a thick sauce, add an uncooked, unpeeled potato. Cook down the liquid until the sauce thickens, about 15 minutes. Try not to overcook it or you'll lose the texture of the tomatoes. Remove the potato.

5. **Chiffonade** the basil. (See "Susie's Rules," page 264 for directions.)

6. **Add** the salt, pepper, basil, and thyme.

7. **Bring** 8 quarts (8 L) water to a boil in a large pot and add 3 tablespoons (45 mL) of salt. The water should taste like the sea. Add the spaghetti and stir frequently with a wooden fork. Follow the instructions on the package, but make sure that you taste for al dente. This should take about 10 minutes.

8. **Add** the drained pasta to the simmering sauce. Stir in the butter and cheese and serve at once.

I like this best made with long-grain Chinese rice that you can buy in Chinatown.

Steamed Chinese Rice

Serves 2

1 cup	long-grain white rice	250 mL
½ tsp	kosher or coarse salt	2 mL
1 Tbsp	butter	15 mL

1. **Rinse** the rice several times until it loses its milky color.

2. **Place** it in a saucepan and gently add cold water. You know that you have added enough water when you can place your index finger on top of the rice and the water level comes to the first joint of your finger.

3. **Add** the salt and butter and bring the rice to a boil.

4. **Cover** and cook over a very, very low heat for 10 to 15 minutes. Check the rice for doneness after 9 minutes.

5. **Drain** and cool.

This rice is best prepared in advance. You can steam it or microwave it to heat (about 2 minutes).

Charley's Fried Rice

Serves 4

1 cup	cooked long-grain white rice, cold	250 mL
1 tsp	peanut oil	5 mL
1	egg	1
1 Tbsp	vegetable oil	15 mL
1/2 cup	green onions, sliced thin	125 mL
1 tsp	chopped ginger	5 mL
1/2	garlic clove, minced	1/2
2 Tbsp	soy sauce	25 mL
1 1/2 Tbsp	sesame oil	7 mL
1/2 cup	peas, frozen or fresh	125 mL
1/4 lb	barbequed pork, diced (best gotten from your favorite Chinese meat store)	125 g
	Kosher or coarse salt to taste (remember, the soy sauce is salty!)	
	Freshly ground pepper to taste	
1/3 cup	chopped cilantro	75 mL

1. **Cook** the rice. (See the recipe for Steamed Rice on page 120.) Refrigerate the cooked rice to cool. I generally make the rice the day before I need it.

2. **Heat** a wok and add the peanut oil.

3. **Scramble** the egg in the hot wok, then dice and set aside.

4. **Reheat** the wok until hot and add vegetable oil. Then add the green onions, and cook for 2 minutes.

5. **Stir** in the ginger and garlic.

6. **Add** the rice, breaking it up with your fingers, and cook until heated through, about 3 minutes.

7. **Add** the soy sauce and sesame oil. Mix through.

8. **Stir** in the peas and the barbequed pork until heated through.

9. **Season** with salt and pepper, then add the cilantro.

Serve immediately.

Risotto can be a bit of a pain to make because it *must* be prepared at the last minute. I am a purist and consequently don't find any "quick" risottos to my liking. However, this recipe is worth the effort. It's simple to make, although it requires about 20 minutes of stirring.

Risotto

Serves 4 as a main course Reduce by half as a side dish for 4		
½ oz	dried porcini mushrooms	15 g
6½ cups	hot chicken stock, homemade preferred, or hot water	1.625 L
6 Tbsp	butter	90 mL
½ lb	mixed fresh wild mushrooms, such as shiitake, chanterelle, porcini, or oyster, trimmed and diced large	250 mL
1	garlic clove, minced	1
3 Tbsp	olive oil	45 mL
1	small onion, minced	1
1½ cups	arborio rice	375 mL
1 cup	white wine	250 mL
¼ cup	minced Italian parsley	50 mL
¼ cup	finely grated Parmigiano-Reggiano cheese	50 mL
1 Tbsp	butter	15 mL
	Kosher or coarse salt and freshly ground pepper to taste	

1. **Soak** the porcini in ¹/₂ cup (125 mL) of the hot stock or water for about 15 minutes. Drain the soaked porcini, straining and reserving the liquid for later use. Rinse them to remove any remaining grit, squeeze them dry, chop, and set aside. Don't overwash. You'll remove much of the great flavor. Just a quick rinse.

2. **Bring** the remaining 6 cups (1.5 L) of stock to a simmer in a medium saucepan over moderate heat. Reduce the heat to very low and cover until ready to use. When I am using my frozen ice cube stocks, I simply put the cubes in a measuring cup in the microwave to defrost and heat through. It saves a step and a pot.

3. In a large heavy saucepan, **melt** 3 tablespoons (45 mL) of the butter over moderately high heat. Add the mushrooms and cook until wilted and lightly browned, about 10 minutes.

4. **Add** the chopped porcini.

5. **Toss in** the garlic, cooking for 2 to 3 minutes.

6. **Transfer** the mushrooms and garlic to a bowl and set aside.

7. **Reduce** the heat to moderate. Add the remaining 3 tablespoons (45 mL) of butter and the olive oil to the saucepan. When the butter is melted, add the onion and cook until softened, about 5 minutes.

8. **Add** the rice and stir to coat each grain well. Increase the heat to moderately high.

9. **Stir in** the white wine and cook, stirring till absorbed.

10. **Add** the strained porcini liquid and about $1/2$ cup (125 mL) of the hot stock and stir constantly until the mixture comes to a simmer.

11. **Add** the hot stock, $1/2$ cup (125 mL) at a time, stirring constantly until the stock is absorbed after each addition. Stir constantly until the rice is tender but still firm and creamy, not soupy, about 15 to 20 minutes longer.

12. **Toss** in the reserved mushrooms, garlic, and and heat through.

13. **Remove** the risotto from the heat and stir in the cheese.

14. **Stir in** the butter. Season to taste with salt and pepper and serve at once.

Meats

When I was a girl, meat was it! Fish was eaten out and was hard-shelled. Pasta meant spaghetti, which was eaten with ketchup and a glob of butter. Eggs were for breakfast and soup wasn't a meal. That left us with meat, the staple the family relied upon. It could also be cooked quickly, a bonus for my working mother.

There isn't a Jewish family holiday that doesn't include brisket. This recipe has been in our family for over 40 years. It must be good. Better yet, leftovers, if there are any, make simply great sandwiches—warm or cold.

Brisket of Beef

Serves 10 to 12

Best made 1 day in advance

¼ cup	corn oil	50 mL
8–10	onions, sliced thinly	8–10
6 lbs	brisket (a kosher meat market is really the best place to buy it whether or not you're Jewish)	3 kg
4	garlic clove, minced	4
1 Tbsp	seasoned salt	15 mL
½ tsp	freshly ground pepper	2 mL
½ tsp	paprika	2 mL

1. **Heat** the oil in a heavy Dutch oven.
2. **Add** the onions and cook them slowly until they are lightly browned.
3. While the onions are cooking, **season** the meat on both sides with the garlic, salt, pepper, and paprika.
4. **Remove** the onions from the pan with a slotted spoon and set aside. Leave behind a slight film of the oil in the pan.
5. **Raise** the heat to sear the seasoned meat on each side until well browned.
6. **Add** the onions back to the pot with the meat, fat side up. Cook covered for 2 hours, turning the meat after 1 hour with tongs. I try never to pierce the skin of poultry or the flesh of meat I'm cooking —I'm convinced it toughens the texture.
7. **Cook,** covered, for another hour.
8. **Remove** the meat from the pan and store in the refrigerator wrapped in foil. Store the gravy in the refrigerator overnight.
9. **Remove** the layer of fat from the cooled gravy and put the gravy into a Dutch oven.
10. **Thinly slice** the beef and add it to the gravy. Cook until warmed through and serve.

Herbed Roast Beef

Serves 8

3	garlic clove, minced	3
1 tsp	chopped fresh thyme or ½ tsp (2 mL) dried thyme	5 mL
1 Tbsp	kosher or coarse salt	15 mL
1 Tbsp	freshly ground black pepper	15 mL
2	bay leaves, crumbled	2
1 Tbsp	olive oil	15 mL
5 lb	standing rib roast	2.5 kg
½ cup	diced onions	125 mL
½ cup	diced carrots	125 mL
½ cup	diced celery	125 mL
½ cup	diced parsnip	125 mL
1 tsp	chopped fresh thyme or ½ tsp (2 mL) dried thyme	5 mL
1 tsp	chopped fresh oregano or ½ tsp (2 mL) dried oregano	5 mL
1	garlic clove, smashed	1

Gravy:

2 Tbsp	all-purpose flour	25 mL
2 cups	beef stock, homemade preferred	500 mL
	Kosher or coarse salt and freshly ground pepper to taste	

(I sometimes cook up a batch of mushrooms and onions and a shallot to add to the cooked and strained gravy.)

1. **Make** a smooth paste of the garlic, thyme, salt, pepper, and crumbled bay leaves mixed with the olive oil. Rub the paste all over the roast.

2. **Transfer** the roast to a rack and set in roasting pan. Marinate, covered, in the refrigerator for at least 8 hours or up to 24 hours. Let the roast stand for 1 hour to come to room temperature.

Preheat the oven to 450°F (230°C)

3. **Place** the roast, rib side down, in the lower middle rack of the oven for 20 minutes. Reduce the heat to 350°F (180°C) and continue to roast.

4. After 1 hour, **strew** the diced vegetables, thyme, oregano, and garlic around the roast and baste with the pan fat.

5. **Roast** until a thermometer inserted into the center of the beef registers 130 °F (54 °C), about 1 1/2 to 1 3/4 hours more.

6. **Remove** the roast to a platter and let it rest for 20 minutes.

For the gravy:

7. **Pour** off all but about 2 tablespoons (25 mL) of the fat.

8. **Press** the cooked vegetables through a fine sieve into the pan.

9. **Whisk** in the flour and cook, scraping up the caramelized bits, until the mixture is deep golden brown, about 3 minutes.

10. **Slowly add** the stock and bring to a boil, stirring until thickened. The gravy should coat the back of a spoon. Add the salt and pepper.

11. **Strain** the gravy to serve.

12. **Remove** the strings from the roast and slice to desired thickness. I prefer 1/2" (1 cm) slices.

Serve with Horseradish Sauce (page 128).

Roasting time chart:	
5-rib roast	2¼ to 2¾ hours
4-rib roast	1¾ to 2¼ hours
3-rib roast	1½ to 1¾ hours
2-rib roast	1 to 1¼ hours

Horseradish Sauce

Serves 6 to 8

1 heaping Tbsp	freshly grated horseradish or 3 Tbsp (45 mL) bottled white hot horseradish	**20 mL**
	Kosher or coarse salt and freshly ground pepper to taste	
	Juice of ½ lemon	
1 cup	heavy (35%) cream, beaten to soft peaks	**250 mL**

1. **Stir** the horseradish, salt, pepper, and lemon juice into the whipped cream.

2. **Refrigerate** until serving.

Rib Steak, the French Way

Serves 2

1 lb	rib steak, 1½"–2" (3.5 cm) thick	**500 g**

Preheat the oven to 400°F (200°C)

1. In a well-heated cast-iron skillet, **brown** the steak about 3 minutes a side.

2. **Pour** off the fat.

3. **Put** into preheated oven for 10 minutes, then turn the meat.

4. **Insert** the tip of an instant-read meat thermometer into the side of the steak. Cook until the temperature is 140°F (60°C) for medium rare, about 5 minutes more.

5. **Remove** from the pan and let the meat rest for 15 minutes before slicing.

I hate to tell you this story for fear that you will not recognize the true depth and breath of Pa's seductive qualities. But I assure you that the man was good. I mean really good.

I would describe him to my friends as being of average height and bald with one eye, but the sexiest man I had ever known. He had to be because he wooed me over a bowl of chili during our first lunch together. Maybe it was because I had never had chili—Mother would not have served such a dish. No wine. No caviar. Just him and the chili. Wow!

Pa's Seductive Chili

Serves 8		
1 lb	ground beef, medium fat	500 g
2 Tbsp	corn oil	25 mL
	Kosher or coarse salt and freshly ground pepper to taste	
1	large onion, diced	1
1	garlic clove, minced	1
2	cans (each 19 oz/540 mL) kidney beans, drained	2
1	can (6 oz/170 mL) tomato paste	1
1 tsp	chili powder	5 mL
1 tsp	paprika	5 mL
1 tsp	Worcestershire sauce	5 mL
½ tsp	hot sauce	2 mL

1. **Brown** the meat in the oil, breaking it up and cooking until the pink disappears.

2. **Drain** the fat.

3. **Add** the salt and pepper to the meat and combine.

4. **Add** the remaining ingredients and simmer, covered, for 90 minutes.

Arthur says, "Stir and taste and add a little water, as needed." Serve with warmed French or Italian bread. Can be frozen for 6 months.

Ellen's Meat Loaf

Serves 4		
3 lbs	ground sirloin	1.5 kg
2	packages dry onion soup mix	2
4	eggs, lightly beaten	4
3 cloves	garlic, minced	3 cloves
2 cups	beef bouillon	500 mL
1 cup	ketchup, or more to taste	250 mL
1/2–3/4 cup	bread crumbs (see page 247)	125–175 mL
	Kosher or coarse salt and freshly ground pepper to taste	
	Corn oil	

Preheat the oven to 350°F (180°C)

1. **Mix** all the ingredients, except the oil, together and put into loaf pan.
2. **Cover** top lightly with corn oil. Bake 1 hour.

Ellen's Hot Meat Loaf Sandwiches

Serves 4		
3 Tbsp	soft butter	45 mL
1	garlic clove, minced	1
4	kaiser rolls	4
4 slices	Ellen's Meat Loaf (above)	4 slices

Preheat the oven to 350°F (180°C)

1. **Mix** the butter and minced garlic with a fork.
2. **Slice** the rolls and spread them with the garlic butter.
3. **Slice** the meat loaf to fit in a roll.
4. **Wrap** each roll in foil and bake for 20 minutes until heated through.

Serve at once.

My sister-in-law Bobby was one of those gentle, fragile, talented people. She was an artist not only at the easel, but at the table as well. She was able to create beautiful spreads that not only looked good, but tasted good. Her great tragedy was that she never knew just how good she was.

Bobby's Flank Steak

Serves 4

1 lb	flank steak, scored	500 g

Marinade:

15 oz	soy sauce	425 mL
2 Tbsp	white vinegar	25 mL
2 Tbsp	brown sugar	25 mL
2	garlic clove, minced	2

1. **Mix** together the marinade ingredients.
2. **Add** the meat and marinate for at least 3 hours.
3. **Broil** or barbecue the steak for about 4 minutes per side.
4. **Remove** and let rest for 10 minutes.
5. **Slice** on the diagonal.

Great served with Ellen's Moroccan Hot Salad (page 63) and Charley's Fried Rice (page 121).

My mother often made this dish when company was coming. It's a bit of a job, but well worth the effort. I have taken some liberties with it, adding garlic, thyme, and a neater approach to the preparation. I know she wouldn't mind.

Grandma Jeanne's Stuffed Cabbage

Makes 18 rolls

1	perfect white cabbage	1

Meat filling:

1	egg, beaten	1
1 cup	hot water	250 mL
2 Tbsp	matzo meal	25 mL
1	white onion, grated	1
3	garlic cloves, minced	3
1 tsp	dried thyme	5 mL
2 Tbsp	long-grain white rice	25 mL
1 ½ lbs	ground beef (not lean)	750 g
	Kosher or coarse salt and freshly ground pepper to taste	

Sauce:

¼ cup	corn or vegetable oil	50 mL
1	white onion, finely diced	1
1 cup	finely diced carrot	250 mL
½ cup	finely diced celery	125 mL
2–3	garlic cloves, minced	2–3
1 cup	tomato sauce	1 cup
1 cup	canned Italian plum tomatoes with their juice	250 mL
1 cup	dry white wine	250 mL
½ tsp	dried thyme	2 mL
	Juice of 1 lemon	
½ cup	orange juice	125 mL
1	can (28 oz/796 mL) apricots (juice and fruit used separately)	1
1 cup	beef consommé	250 mL

	Kosher or coarse salt and freshly ground pepper to taste	
1 tsp	paprika	5 mL
½ cup	brown sugar, or to taste	125 mL
12	sour prunes	12
1 cup	white raisins	250 mL

1. **Blanch** the whole cabbage in salted water to cover. This should take about 5 minutes.

2. **Remove** the cabbage and cool in iced water. Remove the core and very carefully separate the leaves. I drain them on a large towel. Cut away the hard stem of each leaf. You may have to return the cabbage to the water to soften the inner leaves.

For the filling:

3. **Combine** well the egg, water, matzo meal, onion, garlic, thyme, and rice in a large bowl.

4. **Add** the meat, salt, and pepper and mix well with your very, very clean hands. Set aside.

For the sauce:

5. **Pour** the oil into a large, heated Dutch oven. Add the onion to the heated oil and sauté until translucent.

6. **Stir in** the carrot, celery, and garlic, and cook together until the carrots are slightly softened.

7. **Add** the tomato sauce and plum tomatoes, breaking apart the tomatoes with your hands.

8. **Raise** the heat, add the wine to the sauce, and stir until you reduce the liquid by half.

9. **Now stir in** the dried thyme, lemon juice, orange juice, apricot juice, consommé, salt, pepper, paprika, and brown sugar.

10. **Simmer** the sauce, covered, for 1 ¼ hours.

(continues on page 134)

Preheat the oven to 350°F (180°C)

To prepare the 18 cabbage rolls:

11. **Spoon** a very large tablespoon (20 mL) of the meat filling into the center of 1 or 2 leaves. Fold the four sides in to properly enclose the meat in the cabbage.

12. **Add** the apricots, sour prunes, and white raisins to the sauce.

13. **Arrange** the cabbage rolls in the Dutch oven with the sauce. Cover and bake for 1 hour. I prefer to make these a day in advance. They freeze very well.

Owen, my youngest son, is —forgive a Jewish mother— a remarkable man. He is bright, charming, generous, and witty and he treats his women well. I'm rather proud of this fact—it all begins with the mother, you know.

He is the most caring and thoughtful father to his wondrous daughter, Ruby Jeanne.

Owen's great generosity and extravagance come from his grandmother and great-grandfather. I can imagine them gleefully watching him from above as he forks out dollar bills. He may get his intelligence from his father, but his smarts he surely gets from Brooklyn.

He is an adventurous cook, but real stubborn in the kitchen. As I am so forceful and he is so obstinate, we cannot cook together at all. But we do eat together rather well.

Owen, at four, and me.

Owen's Osso Bucco

Serves 6

¼ cup	olive oil	50 mL
6	veal shanks, 2" (5 cm) thick	6
	Kosher or coarse salt and freshly ground pepper	
	Flour for dredging	
1	large onion, finely chopped	1
3	celery stalks, finely chopped	3
2	large carrots, finely chopped	2
2	garlic cloves, minced	2
¾ cup	dry white wine	175 mL
1½ cups	canned Italian plum tomatoes	375 mL
4 cups	hot chicken stock, homemade preferred	1 L

Gremolade:

1 tsp	grated lemon zest	5 mL
1	small garlic clove, minced	1
⅓ cup	chopped Italian parsley	75 mL
2 Tbsp	olive oil	25 mL

1. **Heat** olive oil over medium heat in a heated Dutch oven large enough to hold the veal in a single layer.

2. **Tie** each veal shank with kitchen twine to ensure that it does not come apart in cooking. Just remember to remove the twine before serving.

3. **Season** the veal well with salt and pepper (remember that veal is very bland) and coat it with the flour, shaking off the excess.

4. **Cook** the veal in the hot oil over medium heat, browning on all sides (about 10 to 15 minutes). Remove from the pan and set the veal aside. Don't rush this step, as the veal wants to be nicely browned. It will not only enhance the flavor and the taste; it will hold the shank together through the cooking process.

5. **Add** the onion and garlic to the Dutch oven, stirring frequently.

6. When the onion is translucent, **stir in** the celery and carrots, cooking this mixture until the vegetables are soft, about 15 minutes.

7. **Turn** up the heat, add the wine, and boil, stirring constantly, until the wine has evaporated.

8. **Crush** the tomatoes with your hands as you add them to the pot. Be careful, they have a tendency to explode. Stir in the tomatoes and 2 cups (500 mL) of the hot stock.

9. **Arrange** the veal slices in the casserole and spoon some of the vegetable mixture over them. If the liquid does not cover the meat, add more stock.

10. **Lower** the heat when the liquid comes to a boil, cover the casserole tightly, and simmer gently for 2 hours or until the meat is tender.

11. **Uncover** the casserole to reduce the sauce a bit and cook for about 30 minutes more. I prefer to make the dish to this point the day ahead. Like a stew, it allows the meat to tenderize and really absorb the sauce. Reheat when ready to serve.

12. While the meat is cooking, **chop** the ingredients for the gremolade and combine them.

13. **Remove** the meat to a serving plate 10 minutes before serving and cover with foil to keep warm.

14. **Vigorously boil** the sauce to reduce it a bit more if it is very thin. Stir in the gremolade and simmer for a minute or two. Spoon the sauce over the meat.

This sauce is so good, I often serve it over spaghetti, then place the Osso Bucco on top. Or you can serve the Osso Bucco with Risotto (page 122).

There's a restaurant in Toronto, Sotto Sotto, that my husband and I like to go to. We can walk to it (a definite plus from Pa's point of view). They know us and they treat us well, even when the room is full.

I figure the Veal Nonna on their menu must be made as follows. Arthur, to his credit, insists mine is better than theirs is, but I know better. He would just prefer to eat at home and goes to great lengths to convince me that my home-cooking is better than eating out.

Veal Nonna

Serves 2

1	small eggplant	1
	Kosher or coarse salt	
6 Tbsp	olive oil	90 mL
1	small red onion, diced	1
2	garlic cloves, minced or thinly sliced	2
2	medium carrots, grated	2
2	celery stalks, diced	2
2 Tbsp	fresh thyme or ³/₄ tsp (3 mL) dried thyme	25 mL
1	can (28 oz/796 mL) Italian plum tomatoes, drained	1
	Kosher or coarse salt and freshly ground pepper to taste	
1 Tbsp	fresh basil	15 mL
1 Tbsp	butter	15 mL
4 slices	veal scaloppini	4 slices
12 oz	large mozzarella di bufala cheese, thinly sliced	375 g

Preheat the oven to 350°F (180°C)

1. **Slice** the eggplant thinly and spread on a rack. Sprinkle heavily with coarse salt and let drain for at least 1 hour.

2. **Rinse** very well to remove all traces of the salt and pat dry.

3. **Chiffonade** the basil. (See "Susie's Rules," page 264, for directions.)

4. **Lightly fry** the eggplant in 3 tablespoons (45 mL) of the olive oil until barely brown. Set aside on paper towel to drain.

5. **Add** the diced onion and garlic to 2 tablespoons (25 mL) of cold olive oil, heat slowly, and sauté until translucent, about 10 minutes.

6. **Stir in** the carrots, celery, and thyme and cook for 5 minutes.

7. **Stir in** the tomatoes, salt, pepper, and basil. Cook for about 30 minutes.

8. **Heat** a sauté pan and coat lightly with the remaining 1 tablespoon (15 mL) of olive oil and 1 tablespoon (15 mL) butter. Sauté the veal quickly until just brown, not more than 1 minute a side.

9. **Place** the cooked veal on a lightly oiled baking dish, layer with eggplant, thinly sliced cheese, and tomato sauce.

10. **Bake** until heated through, about 15 minutes.

Liz's Medallions of Lamb

Serves 4		
2	skinless, boneless loins of lamb, about 1½ lbs (250 g)	2
¾ lb	ripe Italian plum tomatoes (about 4)	375 g
12	fresh basil leaves	12
4 Tbsp	olive oil	50 mL
1 tsp	garlic, minced	5 mL
	Kosher or coarse salt and freshly ground pepper to taste	
1 tsp	ground cumin	5 mL
3 Tbsp	butter	45 mL
4	garlic cloves, peeled	4
4 sprigs	fresh thyme or ½ tsp (2 mL) dry thyme	4 sprigs
2 Tbsp	chopped shallots	25 mL
½ cup	water	125 mL

1. **Cut** the lamb into 12 slices.

2. **Peel,** seed, and chop the tomatoes. (See "Susie's Rules," page 267 for peeling tomatoes.) There should be about 1 ½ cups (375 mL).

3. **Chiffonade** the basil. (See "Susie's Rules," page 264 for directions.)

4. **Add** 2 tablespoons (25 mL) of the olive oil to a small saucepan and add the minced garlic to the cold oil. Cook briefly, being careful not to brown the garlic.

5. **Add** the tomatoes, basil, salt, and pepper. Stir and simmer for 5 minutes. You can make this sauce in advance and reheat as needed.

6. **Sprinkle** the lamb with cumin, salt, and pepper.

7. **Heat** the remaining 2 tablespoons (25 mL) of olive oil with 1 tablespoon (15 mL) of butter in a large hot sauté pan.

8. **Add** the lamb, garlic, and thyme. Brown the lamb quickly on all sides and cook over a relatively high heat for about 4 minutes for rare lamb. Remove the lamb to a warm platter.

9. **Add** the shallots to the pan with the garlic cloves and cook briefly, stirring, until wilted.

10. **Add** the water, bring to a boil, and cook for 1 minute.

11. **Add** the remaining 2 tablespoons (25 mL) of butter and any juices that have accumulated around the lamb. Blend well. Taste for seasoning. Remove the garlic cloves.

12. **Divide** the warm tomato sauce equally on four dinner plates. Place three pieces of lamb over the sauce on each plate. Spread some shallot sauce over the lamb.

Here I am, a single mother, with Liz, Andy, and Owen, around 1973.

Rack of Lamb

Serves 4

2	racks of lamb (12 chops in all), fat trimmed from the bones	2

Marinade:

2	long rosemary branches	2
1½ Tbsp	chopped fresh thyme or 2 tsp (10 mL) dried thyme	20 mL
4	garlic cloves, minced	4
4 Tbsp	olive oil	50 mL
1 tsp	freshly ground black pepper	5 mL
	Kosher or coarse salt to taste	
1 tsp	Dijon mustard	5 mL

Bread crumb mixture:

½ cup	fine fresh bread crumbs (see page 247)	125 mL
1½ Tbsp	chopped fresh thyme leaves, or 2 tsp (10 mL) crumbled dried thyme	20 mL
3	medium onions, peeled and cut into wedges	3

1. **Mix** together the rosemary, thyme, garlic, oil, and pepper in a small baking dish, then rub the mixture all over the lamb racks. Cover and refrigerate overnight.

Preheat the oven to 400°F (200°C)

2. **Remove** the lamb from the marinade and season with salt.

3. **Heat** a cast-iron skillet over high heat. When the pan is good and hot, put in the lamb, skin side down, and sear. Then sear on all sides. Make sure you get it nice and brown!

4. **Spread** the fat side of the racks with the mustard. Combine the bread crumbs and the thyme, and pat this mixture evenly over the mustard.

5. **Scatter** the onions in a small roasting pan. Arrange the lamb, ribs side down. Roast in the middle of the oven for 25 minutes or until meat thermometer registers 135°F (57°C) for medium rare.

6. **Set** lamb aside to rest for 15 minutes before serving.

This recipe had its beginnings with a great chef I heard lecture so long ago that he attributed the small number of female chefs to the fact that women couldn't lift the heavy pots.

The chef is gone, so he doesn't know about the female boxers, soldiers, police, and firemen (I know, I know, it should be firepeople, but that just doesn't fit for me).

If it's a lovely summer day, nothing is better than making the lamb on the barbeque. It will take about the same time as the broiler.

Leg of Lamb with Avgolemono Sauce

Serves 6 to 8		
7 lbs	leg of lamb, boned and butterflied	3.5 kg

Seasoning:

2 tsp	kosher or coarse salt	10 mL

Marinade:

²/₃ cup	olive oil	150 mL
3 Tbsp	fresh lemon juice	45 mL
1 tsp	kosher or coarse salt	15 mL
¹/₂ tsp	freshly ground pepper	2 mL
2 Tbsp	coarsely chopped Italian parsley	25 mL
2 tsp	chopped fresh oregano or 1 tsp (5 mL) dried oregano	10 mL
4	bay leaves, coarsely crumbled	4
1 cup	thinly sliced onions	250 mL
3	garlic cloves, minced	3

Avgolemono Sauce:

3	egg yolks	3
1 Tbsp	fresh lemon juice	15 mL
1 tsp	arrowroot	5 mL
1 tsp	kosher or coarse salt	5 mL
¹/₂ tsp	freshly ground pepper	2 mL
¹/₄ tsp	cayenne	1 mL
1 cup	chicken stock, homemade preferred	250 mL
1 Tbsp	finely chopped Italian parsley	15 mL

1. **Combine** the ingredients for the marinade in a large shallow baking dish. Lay the meat in the dish and spoon some of the marinade over it.

(continues on page 144)

143

Cover and refrigerate. Every few hours, turn the meat. Marinate the lamb for at least 12 hours, preferably 24.

2. Without drying the meat, **sprinkle** the fat side first with about a teaspoon (5 mL) of the coarse salt.

3. **Cook** the lamb, either in the broiler, with the rack about 4″ (10 cm) from the heat, or on the barbeque, for about 15 minutes.

4. **Turn** the meat with tongs—not a fork—and sprinkle with the remaining salt. Moisten with a few tablespoons (45 to 50 mL) of the marinade. Because the lamb is so uneven, you will have both well done and rare meat at the end of another 15 minutes.

5. Let the lamb **rest** for 15 to 20 minutes and then slice on an angle.

For the avgolemono sauce:

6. **Combine** the egg yolks, lemon juice, arrowroot, salt, pepper, and cayenne in the top of a double boiler over lightly boiling water.

7. **Beat** together with a wire whisk, and then slowly stir in the cup (250 mL) of stock. Stirring constantly, cook the sauce directly over moderate heat until it begins to thicken. Do not let the sauce boil or you will end up with scrambled eggs. When the sauce clings to the back of a spoon, remove the pot from the heat.

8. **Stir** the chopped parsley into the sauce just before serving.

Serve the lamb with a dab of the sauce on the top.

When I was a girl in Brooklyn, some sixty years ago, the schoolyard was the social center of my world. While I never rushed off to school with great joy, I looked forward to the schoolyard.

It was there I became a master handball player. My friend Arlene and I would consistently beat all comers at the game. Like me, Arlene was built like a stick. At first, other players would assume that these two runts would be an easy mark. Little did they know. We were speedy and mean players. That little black ball would whip like a bullet and we were kings. Oh, so long ago.

The thing that was so comforting about the yard was that there were no social lines. Rich, poor, Christian, Jew—we were all the same. Too young to know any better and still too young to have been taught that there were any differences between us.

There was one problem, though: a class bully named Nathan. He was big and mean, terrifying us all. He wasn't the only bully in my life, however. The other one was my mother. To break her rules was to defy death. One of her house rules was "DO NOT TOUCH MY FOUNTAIN PENS!" Mother was a bookkeeper and used a variety of pens for her work. The pen and the adding machine and her talent were all that she had. The pen was her sword with numbers. These were fountain pens, not ballpoint, not felt tip, but ink pens. You had to dip the point of the pen into a bottle of ink, preferably blue, open and close the gold-plated lever on the base of the pen, and let the pen drink up the ink. Until ballpoint pens came along, everyone had blue fingers and pockets with drips of blue ink.

As I left the house for school one day, incredibly, I broke one of her rules. Lying on the hall table was one of my mother's sacred fountain pens. She'd already left for work, so I felt I was safe in borrowing the pen to impress my school friends. I spent the morning at my desk enthralling my classmates with the workings of this beautiful treasure. I was the envy of all.

It was wartime, and in the knowing certainty that Brooklyn (of all places) would be bombed by the enemy, there were regular air raid drills that took us out of our classrooms. A drill rang on this eventful day. In my haste to leave the classroom, I grabbed the bottom of the pen, leaving the top behind.

When the alarm was over, we went back to our desks and, lo and behold, the top of the borrowed pen was missing. I think that was the first time in my life I was filled with terror. No doubt about it—my mother would kill me.

I searched desperately in, around, and under my desk, but no pen top. I looked again with that feeling in my stomach that only those of you who have done wrong will know. Nausea. Sweat. Faintness.

It was then that one of my classmates told me, "Nathan has the pen top." Nathan the class bully. Horror! I examined all of my bully options and realized I had only one hope.

When school was over, followed by all of my friends, I went over to Nathan in the schoolyard.

"Nathan," I said, "do you have the top of my fountain pen?"

"Yeah."

"Nathan, you give it back to me right this minute."

"Are you kidding? "

"Nathan," I said, "if you don't give me that pen top right now, I'm going to have to hit you."

Try to picture this, my Brooklyn version of the OK Corral. A big, fat, tall, bully of a boy towering over a skinny, terrified little girl. Terrified not only of him, but terrified of the master bully—Mother.

Nathan must have seen this same picture because he laughed. He roared with laughter. I tell you his belly shook. My friends gasped. He laughed some more. My choice was clear. No one frightened me more than my mother. And so, with all the might that fear gives us, I punched the bully Nathan right in the middle of his stomach. It was then I learned about bullies.

Nathan dropped the top of the pen and burst into tears.

Another gasp from my friends.

At this moment, one of the school guards came over to see what the commotion was about.

"She hit me," Nathan said, still crying.

Well, the guard looked at big, fat, tall Nathan and then he looked at skinny little me and he took Nathan by the ear to the principal's office for lying. The pen parts were reunited and returned to the hall table before anyone knew they had been missing.

The morals in this story are too numerous and obvious to mention. Save one. I think that was the first time in my life that I knew about my own power.

The other Nathan is Nathan's in Coney Island at the south end of Brooklyn. Brighton Beach and Aunt Fanny. Fanny, my father's funny-looking older sister, whom everyone said I looked exactly like, lived there too.

Back to Nathan's. The best and only hot dog to eat smothered with mustard and sauerkraut. My mouth waters. The recipe that follows is not meant to ever compete with Nathan's hot dog in a bun.

Grandma Jeanne's Wieners and Beans Casserole

Serves 4		
1	can (14 oz/398 mL) baked beans with molasses or maple syrup	1
6	large hot dogs (knockwurst), cut into bite-size pieces	6
2 Tbsp	dry mustard	25 mL
½ cup	chili sauce	125 mL
¼ cup	brown sugar	50 mL

Preheat the oven to 350°F (180°C)

Place all ingredients in a covered casserole and bake for 1 ½ hours.

So simple and so good.

Poultry

I find myself serving a lot of poultry these days when I entertain. It seems everyone has a worry about cholesterol and won't eat meat. So okay, what about fish? No, no—allergic. No meat—no fish. So here's chicken.

I almost always brine and air-dry my poultry. Please see "Susie's Rules," page 262, for how to do this.

It is best to brine the chicken and then refrigerate on a rack for 4 to 24 hours in the fridge. Makes a crisp skin.

Crispy-Skin Butterflied Chicken

Serves 4

1	whole chicken (3½–4 lbs/ 1.75–2 kg), butterflied	1

Flavored butter:

2 Tbsp	softened butter	25 mL
1	medium garlic clove, minced	1
1 tsp	fresh thyme leaves	5 mL
½ tsp	paprika	2 mL
	Kosher or coarse salt and freshly ground pepper to taste	

1. **Line** the bottom of a broiler pan with foil.
2. **Brine** the chicken. (See "Susie's Rules," page 262, for directions.)
3. **Combine** all the ingredients for the flavored butter.
4. After the chicken has been through the brining process, **gently lift** the skin of the breast and legs. Take the flavored butter and push it under the skin. Then, with the flat of your hand, spread the butter mixture.
5. **Place** the chicken on the broiler rack and refrigerate for 8 to 24 hours to ensure that the chicken will be crisp.

Preheat the oven to 500°F (260°C)

6. **Place** the rack in the middle position of the oven.
7. **Roast** the chicken, breast side down, for 20 minutes. Turn the chicken and continue to roast for about 40 minutes longer. The skin should be crisp and turned a deep brown. An instant-read thermometer should register 190°F (88°C) in the thickest part of the breast.
8. **Let** the chicken rest for 15 minutes on the cutting board and then cut into serving pieces.

I usually buy dark meat quarters, but this recipe can be made using a whole chicken that has been quartered. See "Susie's Rules," page 262, for brining the chicken. Best to brine and then refrigerate on a rack for 4 to 24 hours in the fridge. Makes a crisp skin.

Broiled Lemon Chicken

Serves 4

Marinade:

	Kosher or coarse salt and freshly ground pepper to season	
1 Tbsp	fresh thyme or 1 tsp (5 mL) dried thyme	15 mL
1 Tbsp	fresh oregano or 1 tsp (5 mL) dried oregano	15 mL
2 Tbsp	chopped Italian parsley	25 mL
2	garlic cloves, minced	2
	Juice of 1 lemon	
½ cup	olive oil	125 mL
1	3–4 lb chicken, quartered, or 4 chicken thighs	1

Gremolade:

1	small garlic clove, minced	1
2 Tbsp	chopped Italian parsley	25 mL
1 tsp	finely chopped lemon zest	5 mL
2 Tbsp	olive oil	25 mL

For the marinade:

1. **Combine** the salt, pepper, thyme, oregano, parsley, and garlic in a large bowl. Add the lemon juice and olive oil.

2. **Cover** the chicken pieces well with the marinade and keep covered for at least 2 hours.

Preheat the oven to broil

3. **Adjust** the oven rack to the middle of the oven, not too close to the broiler elements.

4. **Line** a broiler pan with foil and put the chicken on a rack in the pan, skin side down. After about 10 minutes, the chicken will have browned. Turn and brown the skin side well.

5. Reduce the heat to 350°F (180°C) and bake for 45 minutes to 1 hour.

6. While the chicken is baking, **combine** the ingredients for the gremolade. Just before serving, spoon the gremolade over the warm chicken.

Arthur—"Pa"—with his children, Karen and Eric, in the late 1970s.

Chicken Cacciatore

Serves 2		
3	chicken legs, cut into two	3
2	fresh rosemary branches	2
1 tsp	kosher or coarse salt	5 mL
¼ tsp	freshly ground pepper	1 mL
1	garlic clove, minced	1
7 Tbsp	olive oil	95 mL
1	shallot, diced	1
½ cup	diced onion	125 mL
1	large carrot, diced	1
1	celery stalk, diced	1
1 cup	sliced white mushrooms	250 mL
1	red pepper, cut into large dice	1
1	green pepper, cut into large dice	1
¼ cup	chicken stock, homemade preferred	50 mL
½ cup	white wine	125 mL
1 cup	canned Italian plum tomatoes, crushed by hand	250 mL
2 Tbsp	fresh oregano or 1 Tbsp (15 mL) dried oregano	25 mL
½ tsp	red pepper flakes	2 mL

1. **Brine** the chicken. (See "Susie's Rules," page 262, for brining directions.)

2. **Finely mince** the rosemary, salt, pepper, garlic, and 4 tablespoons (50 mL) of the olive oil to make a paste. If you have time, rub the paste over the washed and dried chicken to marinate overnight, covered. If not, marinate for at least 2 hours.

3. **Heat** the remaining olive oil in a heated medium-sized Dutch oven till almost smoking. Brown the chicken pieces well. You may need to do this in batches. Remove the browned chicken to a platter and set aside.

4. **Pour** off all but about 1 tablespoon (15 mL) of the fat in the pan. If it is too browned, pour it all off and add a bit of olive oil.

5. **Sauté** the shallots and onion until slightly browned.

6. **Add** the carrot and celery and cook for 2 to 3 minutes.

7. **Add** the mushrooms and cook until lightly browned.

8. **Add** the peppers. Gently stir until the mixture softens slightly.

9. **Put** the chicken back into the pan and add the stock, white wine, tomatoes, oregano, and red pepper flakes.

10. **Bring** the mixture to a boil. Reduce the heat and cover. Simmer for 1 hour.

Mom and Dad, at Mom's seventy-fifth birthday party, 1979.

Africassee is really a chicken and meatball stew. The flavors are both sweet and sour. While I have given you the recipe for the sauce, I urge you to taste it after an hour of cooking so that you can adjust for sweet or sour. I think you'll need a kosher butcher to get the ingredients.

Chicken Fricassee
(Chicken and Meatball Stew)

Serves 6

Meatballs:

3 slices	French or white bread	3 slices
1 cup	milk	250 mL
1½ lbs	ground beef	750 g
1	egg, lightly beaten	1
1 Tbsp	chopped Italian parsley	15 mL
2	garlic cloves, minced	2
	Kosher or coarse salt and freshly ground pepper to taste	

Stew:

¼ cup	vegetable oil	50 mL
1	onion, diced	1
1	large shallot, diced	1
1	garlic clove, minced	1
2 or 3	celery stalks, with their greens, diced	2 or 3
½	green pepper, diced	½
¾ lb	giblets	375 g
	Kosher or coarse salt and freshly ground pepper to taste	
1 tsp	paprika	5 mL
12	chicken wings, cut in half, remove the tips and freeze for stock	12

Sauce:

⅓ cup	fresh lemon juice	75 mL
2 Tbsp	white vinegar	25 mL
⅓ cup	packed brown sugar	75 mL
1 Tbsp	Worcestershire sauce	15 mL

1	medium-sized bottle of chili sauce	1
2 cups	canned Italian plum tomatoes with their juice	500 mL
1 tsp	kosher or coarse salt	5 mL
½ tsp	freshly ground pepper	2 mL

1. **Soak** the bread in the milk until it is softened. Squeeze the milk out of the bread and mix the bread with the meat, egg, parsley, garlic, salt, and pepper.
2. **Form** the meat into small balls and store on a parchment-lined cookie sheet. Set aside. Don't over-work the balls or press them too firmly. Toughens!
3. **Heat** the oil in a well-heated, cast-iron Dutch oven. Add the onion and sauté over a low heat until softened.
4. **Add** the shallot and garlic to the onion, stirring well. Cook for 5 minutes.
5. **Add** the celery and green pepper to the mixture and cook until softened.
6. **Remove** the onion mixture and set aside.
7. **Raise** the heat in the pan and add oil, if needed.
8. **Add** the giblets and season with salt, pepper, and paprika. Cook until lightly browned, remove from the pan, and set aside.
9. Once again, **add** a bit of oil if needed. Add the wings to the hot pan and season with salt, pepper, and paprika. Turn as they brown.
10. Meanwhile, **mix** together the sauce ingredients.
11. **Add** the vegetables, giblets, meatballs, and the sauce to the pan with the wings. Mixing can be a bit of a trial because you don't want to disturb the meatballs.
12. **Simmer,** covered, for 2 to 3 hours.

I make this dish the day before. Remove the fat that has accumulated before reheating and serving. Freezes nicely!

Okay, here's the skinny on trying to cook Chinese-style. It looks so simple, right? Wrong! You are in the kitchen *hocking*, chopping, slicing, and measuring for hours. Once you have finished getting everything ready to cook, the cooking part becomes real easy. Just throw it into a wok in a certain order and voila! Dinner is ready. All of it in this one pot. But by the time you serve it, your feet are killing you.

Chicken and Peanuts

Serves 4		
1 Tbsp	cornstarch	15 mL
4 Tbsp	soy sauce	50 mL
1 lb	skinless, boneless chicken breast, cut into bite-size pieces	500 g
3	dried hot red chilies, stemmed, seeded, and diced or ½ tsp (2 mL) dried chili flakes	3
5	green onions, cut into ½" (1 cm) slices	5
1	large garlic clove, minced	1
½" piece	ginger, peeled and grated	1 cm piece
3 Tbsp	Chinese rice wine	45 mL
1½ Tbsp	sugar	20 mL
3 Tbsp	chicken stock, homemade preferred	45 mL
3 Tbsp	balsamic vinegar	45 mL
1 Tbsp	sesame oil	15 mL
2 tsp	dark soy sauce	10 mL
3 Tbsp	peanut oil	45 mL
½ cup	shelled skinless peanuts	125 mL

1. **Mix** together the cornstarch and 1 tablespoon (15 mL) of the soy sauce in a medium bowl.

2. **Add** the chicken and coat each piece well. Marinate in the refrigerator, covered, for 30 minutes.

3. **Prepare** the chilies, green onions, garlic, and ginger and set each aside.

4. **Mix** together the remaining 3 tablespoons (45 mL) of the soy sauce and the rice wine, sugar, stock, vinegar, sesame oil, and dark soy sauce. Set aside.

5. **Heat** a wok or large sauté pan until very hot. Add the peanut oil and when it is just beginning to smoke, add the garlic and ginger and sauté quickly.

6. **Add** the marinated chicken and stir-fry for about 3 to 5 minutes or until the chicken is a pale golden color and cooked through.

7. **Add** the chilies for just a moment. Be careful, they can burn.

8. **Toss** with the green onions.

9. **Add** the soy mixture and stir-fry until the sauce thickens, about 3 minutes.

10. **Stir** in the peanuts and serve at once with some Steamed Chinese Rice (page 120).

Trying to describe the problems, anger, jealousy, and love that come with a blended family is a book unto itself. When Arthur and I married, our children were too old to actually blend, but they still had to merge quite a bit. It was hard on all of them, to be sure, but I think the women in the group had a harder time of it than the men. We are, after all, sensitive and emotional and (feminists, forgive me) difficult.

My stepdaughter, Karen, and I had a rather rocky relationship from the get-go. Each of us would try, in our way, to please the other, but often it was to no avail. I believe we sincerely wanted our relationship to work, but for many years we were distanced. It was hard on all of us. Now, I guess, we have all finally grown up and peace exists in the valley.

Here is Karen's favorite family recipe. It is best to brine the chicken and then refrigerate on a rack for 4 to 24 hours in the fridge. Makes a crisp skin.

Karen's Maple Syrup Chicken

Serves 4 (recipe can be doubled for 8)

1	4 lb (2 kg) chicken, cut into pieces	1
½ cup	vegetable oil	125 mL
¼ cup	white or red wine vinegar	50 mL
1 Tbsp	soy sauce	15 mL
1 Tbsp	finely chopped ginger	15 mL
2	garlic cloves, minced	2
¼ cup	pure maple syrup	50 mL
2 Tbsp	fresh lemon juice	25 mL

Sauce:

¼ cup	pure maple syrup	125 mL
3 Tbsp	butter	45 mL
1 Tbsp	soy sauce	15 mL
1	garlic clove, chopped	1
	Kosher or coarse salt	
¼ tsp	cayenne pepper	1 mL

1. **Brine** the chicken. (See "Susie's Rules," page 262, for directions.)

2. **Make** a marinade from the oil, vinegar, soy sauce, ginger, garlic, maple syrup, and lemon juice.

3. **Put** the chicken in a large container and pour the sauce over it. Cover and refrigerate for up to 24 hours, turning periodically.

Preheat the oven to 400°F (200°C)

4. **Put** the chicken pieces in a baking dish and bake for about 45 minutes or until done. Baste several times with the pan juices and any leftover marinade.

5. While the chicken is cooking, **prepare** the sauce. Combine the maple syrup, butter, soy sauce, and garlic in a small saucepan and bring to a boil. Reduce the heat and simmer until the sauce is thickened and reduced by half.

6. **Season** with salt and cayenne pepper.

7. **Pour** this sauce over the chicken to serve.

Karen likes it with rice or angel-hair pasta.

No matter the bird of choice, I season them all the same way and then stuff them with my mother's Ritz cracker stuffing, the recipe for which follows. Best to brine the poultry and then refrigerate it on a rack for 4 to 24 hours. Makes a crisp skin. See "Susie's Rules," page 262, for brining poultry.

Roast Capon, Chicken, or Turkey

Preheat the oven to 400°F (200°C)

Serves 4

1	4 lb (2 kg) bird	1
1 Tbsp	seasoned salt	15 mL
½ tsp	freshly ground pepper	2 mL
1	garlic clove, minced	1
2 tsp	paprika	10 mL
1 Tbsp	softened butter	15 mL
1 cup	Pepsi, Coca Cola, or orange juice for basting	250 mL

1. **Mix** the salt, pepper, garlic, and paprika with a bit of water to create a paste.

2. **Rub** the poultry with softened butter and then spread the herb mixture over the skin. Stuff or not.

3. **Place** the bird on a rack in a roasting pan, breast side down, and roast for 15 minutes.

4. **Reduce** the heat to 350°F (180°C).

5. **Pour** the cola or juice over the bird and turn breast side up. Remember not to pierce the skin.

6. **Baste** every 20 minutes, QUICKLY, since the oven will cool off if the door is open too long. (See the note on basting in "Susie's Rules," page 262.)

7. **Bake** an unstuffed bird for 20 minutes per pound, a stuffed one 25 minutes per pound.

Let the bird rest for about 20 minutes before carving.

Thanksgiving in Brooklyn in the 1940s. Dad is carving and Mom is trying to look like a sweet and docile "little woman." Don't believe a word!

Ritz Cracker Stuffing

To stuff a 4 lb (2 kg) bird. Adjust for a larger bird.		
3 Tbsp	corn oil	45 mL
1	onion, diced	1
2	celery stalks, diced	2
½	large green pepper, diced	½
2 cups	Ritz Crackers, lightly crumbled	500 mL
1	egg, lightly beaten	1
	Kosher or coarse salt and freshly ground pepper to taste	

1. **Heat** the oil in a large heated sauté pan. Add the onions and cook until translucent.

2. **Add** the celery and green pepper and cook for another 15 minutes on low heat or until the vegetables have softened.

3. **Remove** the ingredients from the heat to cool.

4. Just before you are ready to stuff your bird, **combine** the Ritz crackers, egg, salt, and pepper in a large bowl.

5. **Add** the cooked ingredients and mix through.

6. If the stuffing is too dry, **add** a bit of water to the combined ingredients.

I also stuff the neck cavity and close securely.

This is not merely a sandwich, it is an experience of tastes and textures. For lunch or dinner with a bowl of tomato soup, c'est tout. It's one of Suzanne's recipes. She made it up as she went along, pulling ingredients from her fridge. This was before Somersizing.

Chicken Sandwich

Serves 2

1	chicken breast, skin and bone removed	1
1	garlic clove, minced	1
½ **tsp**	dried thyme	2 mL
½ **tsp**	dried oregano	2 mL
¼ **cup**	chopped parsley	50 mL
	Kosher or coarse salt and freshly ground pepper to taste	
	Olive oil	
½	lemon	½
7 slices	eggplant, washed	**7 slices**
1	red pepper	1
½	red onion	½
1	French baguette cut into 2 (6"/15 cm) pieces	1
	Mayonnaise, homemade preferred (see page 248)	

1. **Put** the chicken in a bowl and season on both sides with the garlic, thyme, oregano, parsley, salt, and pepper.

2. **Sprinkle** with olive oil and cover the bowl to refrigerate for 2 to 24 hours. Longer is better. It is always good to turn the poultry in the marinade.

3. An hour before preparation, **squeeze** the lemon over the chicken.

4. **Place** the eggplant slices on a rack or colander. Salt well with kosher or coarse salt and allow to drain for 1 hour.

Preheat the grill or the broiler

5. **Grill** or broil the chicken 6 minutes a side. Test for doneness.

6. **Rinse** the eggplant thoroughly (don't leave any salt behind) and pat dry.

7. **Lightly brush** the eggplant with olive oil and grill on each side.

8. **Roast** and peel the pepper. (See "Susie's Rules," page 265, for directions.)

9. **Slice** the roasted pepper into long pieces.

10. **Thinly slice** the red onion.

11. **Slice** the baguettes in half. (I always heat my very lightly dampened baguette in the oven for a few minutes and, after slicing it, I remove much of the dough. Makes for a crustier sandwich that you can get your mouth around.) Slather some mayo on the top and bottom of the bread.

12. **Slice** the chicken 1/4″ (0.5 cm) thick.

13. **Build** your sandwich with the chicken, pepper, onion, and eggplant. Cut each sandwich in half.

I love seeing men in my kitchen: my son-in-law, Doug (left), and my son Owen.

Whenever I am in England a must-stop is Fortnum and Masons for their chicken sandwich. No complicated taste sensations here. Just good chicken and good mayo.

The Best Brit Chick Sandwich

Serves 2		
1	chicken breast	1
	Chicken stock, homemade preferred	
1	small shallot	1
1	celery stalk cut in two	1
	Kosher or coarse salt and freshly ground pepper to taste	
4 slices	white bread	4 slices
2 handfuls	bean sprouts	2 handfuls
	Creamy Yummy Mayonnaise (see page 248)	

1. **Cover** the breast with chicken stock in a medium saucepan.

2. As the stock boils, **remove** the fat and scum that rise to the top.

3. **Add** the shallot, celery, salt, and pepper. Simmer for about 30 minutes or until the chicken is cooked through. Cool.

4. **Slice** the chicken into $1/4''$ (0.5 cm) thick slices.

5. **Remove** the crusts from the bread and cover thickly with the mayonnaise.

6. **Build** the sandwich with the sliced chicken and bean sprouts.

7. **Quarter** each sandwich to serve.

Drinking was not a big item with second-generation New York Jews. Money was not to be squandered on such a thing. It was for a house, an education for your children, and food.

On Saturday nights when I was a girl, my parents' friends would have their weekly card games. There were five couples and the games would alternate from house to house. Drinks were served before the games began, followed by a late supper after the games were over. The suppers were prepared to out-rival the previous week's offerings. As time went by, these meals became more and more elaborate. I have a vivid memory of my hand being slapped as I tried to snitch a prune that was stuffed with a strawberry. I have no idea where Mother got that idea from, but the next morning they were all gone.

The mornings after were filled with the smell of cigars and cigarettes. Everything was put away in its place and the rug properly carpet-swept. The whiskey bottles might still be out, but one knew that they were *verboten*.

So alcohol became something for celebrations and primarily for the older folks. When I went off to Syracuse University, and my first taste of freedom, I started to drink beer. Never could bear the bitter taste. I felt much the same about hard liquor and would drink mine straight, so as to get it over with as quickly as possible. My father was quite horrified when he learned that, although I could hold my liquor, I would order a glass of milk with my dessert, not coffee. No self-respecting drinker would do such a thing.

When my parents retired and moved south, their drinking rhythm changed. On one of my visits with Liz, Andy, and Owen we were out for dinner every night.

"Dad," I said, "we don't have to eat out every night. It's very expensive."

"Worth every penny," he said. "You see, Susie, 'party time' begins with drinks at 5:00 every evening. If we are eating at home, Mother has one drink and then she'll start making supper. After supper it's 'GEORGE, sweep the floor!' 'GEORGE, put this away!' 'GEORGE, take the garbage out!' But when we go out for dinner, Mother still has one drink at home and then when we get to the restaurant, she'll have another. Then, after dinner, in her softest, sweetest voice it's, "George, take me home, dear."

We are dealing with a woman who was a real *tsotska*. A pistol! By the way, she was still flirting with and seducing my father when she was in her late seventies. I salute her and my parents heated relationship with this dish.

Southern Fried Chicken

Serves 4		
1	4 lb (2 kg) chicken, cut into small pieces (I usually cut 12 to 16 pieces, or use 4 legs and thighs cut into small pieces)	1
	Milk	
1½ cups	all-purpose flour	375 mL
¾ cup	corn flake crumbs	175 mL
½ cup	fresh bread crumbs (see page 247)	125 mL
1 tsp	seasoned salt	5 mL
½ tsp	freshly ground pepper	2 mL
½ tsp	paprika	2 mL
2	eggs, beaten	2
½ cup	corn oil	125 mL
½ cup	shortening	125 mL

1. **Brine** the chicken. (See "Susie's Rules," page 262, for directions.) After brining the chicken, rinse it well to remove all taste of the brining salt.

2. **Put** the chicken in a large bowl and cover it with milk.

3. **Refrigerate** for at least several hours or overnight.

4. **Mix** all the dry ingredients together in a plastic bag and shake to mix well.

5. **Beat** the eggs in a medium bowl.

6. **Dip** two or three of the chicken pieces at a time into the egg and then place in plastic bag, shaking to coat well.

7. **Place** the chicken on a large rack over a cookie sheet and refrigerate for at least 3 hours.

8. **Heat** the corn oil and shortening in a heated frying pan, preferably electric or cast-iron, until the oil is quite hot. The hotter the oil, the less will be absorbed into the chicken.

9. **Arrange** the chicken in the pan, skin side down, and cook until nicely browned. Do about four or five pieces at a time so that the fat does not cool down.

10. **Turn** the chicken pieces and cook the reverse side until browned.

11. **Carefully place** the chicken pieces on several layers of paper towel to remove excess oil. I often change the paper towel at least twice to make sure I remove as much oil as possible, turning the chicken to drain it well.

12. **Refrigerate** the chicken now for as much as 24 hours before baking.

Preheat the oven to 350°F (180°C)

13. **Bake** the chicken for 45 minutes.

Serve warm or cool. Really good with Pickled Watermelon Rind (page 251) and New Potato Salad with Herbs and Shallots (page 56).

Arthur's sister, Halina, is another of the women of my generation who were good girls. We did what was expected and never really caused any trouble. You see, we had so few options that we really couldn't do anything wrong. The expectations included going to school, getting married, and having three children. I remember, when I was applying to university, asking my mother her advice about what subject I should major in. Her reply: "What difference does it make, you'll get married after school anyway."

Halina did the expected thing and ran a household that involved constant entertaining in support of her husband's position at the University of Michigan. No question that she did it well, but I suspect she thought that maybe there was more out there that she was missing. Were she born today, it would be hard to imagine what she'd grow up to be. Surely a business-woman. Absolutely a success.

Halina's Duck

Serves 4 (or cut the recipe in half for 2)		
2	whole ducks	2
3 cups	soy sauce	750 mL
6 cups	water	1.5 L
8	green onions, sliced in half	8
	Hoisin sauce	

1. **Discard** any large pieces of fat from the duck cavities.

2. **Trim** off the wing tips.

3. **Season** the cavities with salt and pepper to taste.

4. **Pierce** the duck skin well all over. Insert the tip of a very pointed, sharp knife into the skin only, being careful not to cut into the flesh.

5. **Place** the ducks in a large pot and cover with the soy sauce, water, and green onions.

6. **Boil,** covered, for $1^1/2$ to $13/4$ hours, turning as you cook to ensure that the duck is always covered with the liquid.

7. **Cool** the ducks in the pot until room temperature, or until you can handle them with your hands.

8. **Remove** the ducks from the cooking liquid, saving 1 cup (250 mL) of the broth.

Preheat the oven to 325°F (160°C)

9. **Pour** the reserved 1 cup (250 mL) of the duck broth into a roasting pan.

10. **Cut** the duck into quarters or eighths and bake on a rack for 1 hour, basting occasionally with the juices from the pan.

11. **Place** under the broiler to brown.

Serve with the hoisin sauce as a condiment.

I never really loved duck until I found this recipe. My father always ordered duck at French restaurants, but it seemed too exotic and fatty for my taste. This recipe removes all the fat and offers up a really crisp, moist duck. I'd serve it with the orange sauce on page 172. Best to brine the duck and then refrigerate on a rack for 4 to 24 hours in the fridge. Makes a crisp skin. See "Susie's Rules," page 262, for brining poultry.

Four-Hour Roast Duck

Serves 2		
1	duck, brined and air-dried	1
	Kosher or coarse salt and freshly ground pepper to taste	
3	garlic cloves, peeled and chopped	3
½ **bunch**	fresh thyme	½ **bunch**
1 cup	white wine	**250 mL**

Preheat the oven to 250°F (120°C)

1. **Discard** any large pieces of fat from the duck cavity.

2. **Trim** off the wing tips.

3. **Season** the cavity with salt and pepper to taste, then rub it with the garlic, and leave the garlic in the duck.

4. **Stuff** the cavity with sprigs of thyme.

5. **Pierce** the duck skin well all over. Insert the tip of a very pointed, sharp knife into the skin only, being careful not to cut into the flesh.

6. **Set** a rack in the middle of the oven.

7. **Place** the duck, breast side up, on a rack set on a shallow roasting pan. Remove the duck from the oven every hour, piercing the skin on both sides with a paring knife, as described above. Turn the duck and pour off the fat.

8. After 2 hours, **add** the white wine to the pan drippings. Continue roasting for an additional hour, for a total of 3 hours.

9. **Increase** the oven temperature to 300 °F (150 °C).

10. **Season** the duck skin with salt and pepper and cook until the skin is crisp and browned, 1 hour more.

11. **Reserve** 2 tablespoons (25 mL) of the duck drippings for the orange sauce.

12. Allow the duck to **rest** for 20 minutes before serving.

13. **Cut** the duck into four pieces.

Serve with Sauce l'Orange (page 172).

Sauce l'Orange

Serves 2		
4	navel oranges	4
½ cup	granulated sugar	125 mL
½ cup	water	125 mL
2 Tbsp	duck pan drippings	25 mL
1 cup	fresh orange juice	250 mL
¼ cup	fresh lemon juice	50 mL
¼ cup	brandy	50 mL
3 Tbsp	cornstarch	45 mL
	Kosher or coarse salt and freshly ground pepper to taste	

1. **Carefully cut** the rind from the oranges. I use a vegetable peeler.

2. **Finely mince** the rind in a mini–food processor.

3. **Place** the rind in a small saucepan and cover with water. Boil for about 3 minutes. Drain and set aside.

4. **Heat** the sugar and water in a saucepan, then boil, uncovered, until the syrup is a light caramel color.

5. **Add** 2 tablespoons (25 mL) of the duck pan drippings, and the orange rind and juice, lemon juice, and brandy.

6. **Boil** uncovered until the sauce has reduced a little. At this point the sauce can be set aside.

7. **Make** a paste with the cornstarch mixed with 5 tablespoons (75 mL) of the sauce.

8. **Slowly add** this mixture a tablespoon (15 mL) at a time to the sauce until the right consistency is achieved.

9. **Heat** through and season to taste with salt and pepper. Pour into a sauceboat to serve with duck.

10. **Cut** all the white pith from the oranges and slice the fruit into $1/4''$ (0.5 cm) thick circles and serve with the duck as well.

Vegetables

Vegetables are one of the reasons I wish I lived in California rather than Toronto. On the West Coast there is an abundance of fresh and unusual vegetables all year round. Instead, in Toronto, I live with cardboard vegetables for too much of the year. I am a "fresh anything" freak and with good cause. Life has taught me fresh is best.

Asparagus with Hollandaise Sauce

Serves 4

24–30	asparagus spears	24–30

Hollandaise sauce:

3	egg yolks	3
1½ Tbsp	fresh lemon juice	20 mL
⅛ tsp	cayenne pepper	0.5 mL
¼ tsp	kosher or coarse salt	1 mL
½ cup	bubbling butter	125 mL

1. **Prepare** and cook the asparagus until slightly al dente (See "Susie's Rules," page 262, for preparing and cooking asparagus.)

For the Hollandaise sauce:

2. **Put** all the ingredients, except the butter, in a blender.

3. **Mix** slightly.

4. **Very, very, very slowly pour** in the hot butter and blend until the sauce is thick and smooth. Serve over warm asparagus.

Asparagus with Vinaigrette

Serves 4

24–30	asparagus spears	24–30
1	hard-boiled egg	1

Vinaigrette:

3 Tbsp	finely minced shallots	45 mL
3 Tbsp	sherry vinegar	45 mL
¼ tsp	Dijon mustard	1 mL
2 tsp	finely chopped fresh tarragon	10 mL
1 Tbsp	fresh lemon juice	15 mL
⅓ cup	olive oil	75 mL

Kosher or coarse salt and freshly ground pepper to taste

1. **Prepare** and cook the asparagus as above. Cool to room temperature.

2. **Grate** the egg into a small bowl and set aside.

3. **Mix** all the ingredients for the vinaigrette.

4. **Toss** the asparagus with 2 tablespoons (25 mL) of the vinaigrette.

5. **Drizzle** the remaining vinaigrette over the asparagus and top with the grated egg.

Serve immediately.

This method can also be used for broccoli or Brussels sprouts.

Arthur's Cauliflower with Burnt Bread Crumbs

Serves 4		
½ head	cauliflower, cored, washed, and broken into serving-size pieces	½ head
3 Tbsp	kosher or coarse salt	45 mL
3 Tbsp	butter	45 mL
¼ cup	fresh bread crumbs (see page 247)	50 mL
1 Tbsp	kosher or coarse salt and freshly ground pepper to taste	15 mL

1. **Put** the cauliflower in a pot of salted cold water to cover.

2. **Bring** to a boil, uncovered, for about 15 minutes. Test with a fork to ensure the vegetable is still firm, but not hard. Drain.

3. **Put** the cauliflower back into the pot on low heat to remove all the moisture. Shake the pot to prevent sticking.

4. **Melt** the butter in a small sauté pan and add the bread crumbs. You may need to add a bit more butter to ensure that the mixture is not too dry.

5. When this mixture is bordering on burnt, **add** it to the cauliflower. Season with salt and pepper and serve.

This dish makes for a delicious lunch or supper.

Corn Fritters

Serves 8		
1 cup	all-purpose flour	250 mL
2 tsp	kosher or coarse salt	10 mL
½ tsp	freshly ground pepper	2 mL
1¼ tsp	baking powder	6 mL
⅔ cup	milk	175 mL
1	egg	1
2 Tbsp	melted butter	25 mL
8	ears corn	8
½ cup	minced green onion	125 mL
½ cup	diced red pepper	125 mL
2	medium jalapeno peppers, minced	2
¼ tsp	Tabasco sauce	1 mL
	Vegetable oil	

1. **Combine** the flour, salt, pepper, and baking powder in a large bowl.

2. **Combine** the milk, egg, and melted butter in another small bowl.

3. **Add** the wet ingredients to the dry ingredients.

4. **Remove** the husks and silks from the corn and cut the kernels off the cobs.

5. **Fold** the corn, green onion, pepper, jalapenos, and Tabasco sauce into the batter mixture until incorporated.

6. **Fry** the fritters in a hot sauté pan in ½″ (1 cm) hot vegetable oil.

7. **Remove** the fritters from the oil with a slotted spoon and drain on paper towel.

Serve with sour cream and tomato salsa.

Baked Eggplant Casserole

Serves 2 to 4

2 Tbsp	olive oil for frying	25 mL
1	medium onion, diced	
1	small carrot, peeled and diced	1
1	small celery stalk with leaves, diced	1
3 Tbsp	minced Italian parsley	45 mL
1 Tbsp	fresh oregano or 1 tsp (5 mL) dried oregano	15 mL
1/3 cup	chopped fresh basil	75 mL
1 Tbsp	fresh thyme or 1 tsp (5 mL) dried thyme	15 mL
1	large garlic clove, minced	1
1	can (28 oz/796 mL) Italian plum tomatoes, well-drained and chopped	1
1/2 cup	dry red wine	125 mL
	Kosher or coarse salt and freshly ground pepper to taste	
1/2 tsp	granulated sugar	2 mL
1	large eggplant (about 1 lb/500 g), preferably Sicilian	
	Kosher or coarse salt	
2	eggs, well-beaten	2
2 cups	bread crumbs (see page 247) seasoned with thyme, oregano and bit of grated Parmigiano-Reggiano cheese	500 mL
2 Tbsp	olive oil	25 mL
2 cups	grated mozzarella cheese (mozzarella di bufalo is quite nice here)	500 mL
1/2 cup	grated Parmigiano-Reggiano cheese	125 mL
1 cup	grated Romano cheese	250 mL
1/3 cup	grated Asiago cheese	75 mL
2 Tbsp	butter	25 mL

Preheat the oven to 350°F (180°C)

1. **Heat** the oil in a heated saucepan over medium heat.

2. **Add** the onions and cook until translucent, about 10 minutes.

3. **Add** the carrot, celery, and parsley.

4. **Sauté,** stirring often, for an additional 10 to 15 minutes until the vegetables are golden.

(continues on page 178)

177

5. **Add** the herbs and garlic, and then the tomatoes, crushing them in your hands as you put them in the pot. Be careful, they can spit.

6. **Add** the red wine, salt, pepper, and sugar.

7. **Simmer,** uncovered, for about 15 minutes or until the sauce thickens. The sauce can be made up to 3 or 4 days in advance.

8. **Peel** the eggplant and slice into $1/4''$ (0.5 cm) slices.

9. **Sprinkle** with coarse salt, place in a colander, and drain for about 30 minutes.

10. **Rinse** the eggplant very well to remove all traces of the salt and pat the eggplant thoroughly dry. Place between layers of paper towel and put something heavy over the eggplant to press it down for about 1 hour.

11. **Dip** each slice of eggplant into the beaten eggs and then into the bread crumbs.

12. **Heat** the oil in a large heated sauté pan and fry the eggplant slices until well browned on both sides. Drain on paper towels.

13. **Spoon** $1/2$ cup (125 mL) of the sauce to coat the bottom of a well-greased $10''$ x $10''$ (25 cm x 25 cm) baking dish (preferably one that you can bring to the table).

14. **Add** 3 or 4 eggplant slices.

15. **Cover** with a layer of grated mozzarella cheese and a sprinkling of the other grated cheeses.

16. **Repeat** the layers, ending with a layer of cheese.

17. **Sprinkle** the top with the remaining cheese, including the asiago and parmesan, and a dab of butter. Don't put any mozzarella on the top, as it will dry out too much in the baking.

18. **Bake** for 20 to 25 minutes or until the mixture is bubbling and brown.

19. **Allow** to cool for 10 minutes before serving.

This can be made ahead and baked just before serving.

This simple middle-Eastern dish requires only eggplant, garlic oil, and an appetite. The darker you fry the vegetable, the deeper the flavor.

Fried Eggplant

Serves 2 (depending on the size of the eggplant)		
1	small eggplant	1
2 Tbsp	kosher or coarse salt	25 mL
½ cup	olive oil	125 mL
1–2	garlic cloves, minced	1–2
1 Tbsp	chopped fresh parsley	15 mL

1. **Slice** the unpeeled eggplant $1/4''$ (0.5 cm) thick.

2. **Lay out** on wire rack and sprinkle both sides well with salt. Let the eggplant rest for about 20 minutes.

3. Wash each slice well to ensure that you remove all the salt from the eggplant. Pat each piece dry.

4. **Heat** the oil in a large, heated sauté pan until almost smoking. Add the eggplant and garlic and sauté until each slice of eggplant is well browned. Turn the eggplant slices and repeat on the underside. Watch that the garlic does not burn.

Serve hot, sprinkled with the chopped parsley.

This recipe works well as a first course or as a side dish.

Eggplant Manicotti with Tomato Sauce

Makes 36 rolls

3	large eggplants	3
	Kosher or coarse salt	
	Olive oil	

Filling:

2 cups	ricotta cheese	500 mL
1/4 cup	Parmigiano-Reggiano cheese, grated, or more to taste	50 mL
2	egg yolks, beaten	2
	Kosher or coarse salt and freshly ground pepper to taste	
Dash	freshly grated nutmeg	Dash
1 large bunch	fresh spinach, stemmed	1 large bunch

Tomato sauce:

1 bunch	basil leaves	1 bunch
2 Tbsp	olive oil	25 mL
1 cup	chopped onions	250 mL
1 cup	chopped carrots	250 mL
1 cup	chopped celery	250 mL
2 Tbsp	granulated sugar	25 mL
3/4 tsp	kosher or coarse salt	3 mL
1/2 tsp	freshly ground pepper	2 mL
4 lbs	Italian plum tomatoes, quartered	2 kg
1/2 cup	heavy cream	125 mL

For the filling:

1. **Combine** the ricotta and Parmigiano-Reggiano cheese and stir to mix.
2. **Stir** in the egg yolks, which will hold the mixture together.
3. **Add** the salt, pepper, and grated nutmeg.
4. **Set** aside in the refrigerator.
5. **Wash** the spinach and do not drain.
6. **Steam** the spinach in a saucepan until just wilted, but not cooked through, about 4 minutes.

7. **Drain** thoroughly and squeeze the water from the spinach. Pat completely dry with paper towels.

8. **Chop** finely and drain again.

9. **Stir** into the ricotta mixture and set aside.

Preheat the oven to 350°F (180°C)

10. **Peel** and slice the eggplants lengthwise into $1/4$" (0.5 cm) slices.

11. **Place** in colander, sprinkle with salt, and let drain for 30 minutes.

12. **Rinse** thoroughly to remove all the salt and dry with paper towels.

13. **Place** the eggplant slices in a lightly oiled baking pan or sheet.

14. **Sprinkle** with a bit of olive oil and bake for 15 to 20 minutes, until barely cooked. Cool slightly.

15. **Put** 1 tablespoon (15 mL) of the ricotta mixture into the end of a slice of eggplant and roll the slice to form a manicotti-like tube. Repeat with the remaining eggplant slices. (These can be prepared in advance and refrigerated.)

16. **Place** on a lightly oiled baking sheet and bake for 20 to 30 minutes.

While the eggplant is baking, prepare the tomato sauce:

17. **Chiffonade** the basil. (See "Susie's Rules," page 264, for directions.)

18. **Pour** the olive oil into a heated sauté pan.

19. **Cook** the onion in the oil until translucent.

20. **Add** the carrots and celery to the onions, cooking until just tender.

21. **Add** the sugar, salt, and pepper.

22. **Stir in** the tomatoes and simmer for about 1 hour or until most of the tomato juice has boiled away.

(continues on page 182)

23. **Cool** slightly and run through a food mill.

24. **Return** to a low heat to reduce the purée by about a third.

25. **Stir** in the heavy cream. Simmer for 10 to 15 minutes.

26. **Spoon** a bit of the sauce on a plate and then top with three of the eggplant-ricotta rolls. Ribbon on more sauce and garnish with the basil chiffonade.

Do I look happy or what? Arthur and me on our wedding day, September 1981.

These capers are *great* tossed onto a salad, or over fish or veggies.

Fried Capers

Makes about ½ cup (125 mL)		
¼ cup	olive oil	50 mL
½ cup	capers, well-drained and dried	125 mL

1. **Heat** the oil in a hot sauté pan and add the capers.

2. **Cook** over high heat, stirring occasionally, until browned. This takes about 2 or 3 minutes. Do be careful—they spit a bit.

3. **Drain** on paper towel and serve immediately.

Roasted Carrots

Serves 8 as a side dish		
2 lbs	baby carrots	1 kg
2 Tbsp	olive oil	25 mL
½ tsp	kosher or coarse salt	2 mL
¼ tsp	freshly ground pepper	1 mL

Preheat the oven to 475°F (240°C)

1. **Toss** the carrots, oil, salt, and pepper in a foil-lined broiler pan and spread out in a single layer.

2. **Roast** in the middle position of the oven for 12 minutes.

3. **Shake** the pan to toss the carrots and continue roasting for another 8 minutes or so, shaking the pan two more times, or until carrots are browned and tender.

Roasted Maple Carrots with Browned Butter

Serves 8 as a side dish

2 lbs	baby carrots	1 kg
1½ Tbsp	olive oil	20 mL
½ tsp	kosher or coarse salt	2 mL
¼ tsp	freshly ground pepper	1 mL

Sauce:

2 Tbsp	butter	25 mL
2 Tbsp	maple syrup	25 mL

Preheat oven to 475°F (240°C)

1. **Toss** the carrots, oil, salt, and pepper in a foil-lined broiler pan and spread out in a single layer.

2. **Roast** in the middle position of the oven for 10 minutes.

3. While the carrots are roasting, **prepare** the sauce. Heat the butter in a small saucepan over medium heat until a deep gold color, about 1 minute. Watch closely—you want to brown and not burn the butter.

4. **Remove** the pan from the heat, stir in the maple syrup, and drizzle the mixture over the carrots.

5. **Shake** the pan to toss the carrots and continue roasting, shaking the pan two more times, for another 8 minutes, or until carrots are browned and tender.

Frenched Green Beans with Burnt Butter

Allow 1 handful of green beans per person

	Green beans	
	Kosher or coarse salt and freshly ground pepper	
1 Tbsp per serving	butter	15 mL per serving

1. **Rinse** the beans under cold water.

2. **Remove** the stems and french the beans. You can do this either with a "frenching" instrument or by slicing the beans very, very thinly with a sharp knife.

3. **Bring** 6 quarts (6 L) of water to a boil in a large sauce pan. Add 2 tablespoons of salt. The water should taste like the sea.

4. **Add** the prepared beans to the boiling water and cover the pot. Cook the beans until they are al dente. Start checking after 4 minutes.

5. **Drain** the beans and put them in a large bowl of ice water immediately to cool and to prevent the beans from losing their lovely green color.

6. When you are ready to serve, **drain** the beans and dry them well.

7. **Heat** the butter in the saucepan you boiled the beans in until quite brown. Toss the beans with the butter and season with salt and pepper.

Serve at once.

A delicious first course or side dish.

Stuffed Red Peppers

Serves 4 (recipe can be doubled)

4	perfect red or yellow peppers	4
1½ lbs	mozzarella cheese, diced or shredded	750 g
1 Tbsp	chopped fresh oregano	15 mL
1 Tbsp	chopped fresh thyme	15 mL
1	egg	1
1 cup	fresh bread crumbs (see page 247)	250 mL
	Kosher or coarse salt and freshly ground pepper to taste	
	Olive oil	

Preheat the oven to 350°F (180°C)

1. **Cook** and gently core the peppers, keeping them whole for stuffing. (See "Susie's Rules," page 265, for roasting and peeling peppers.)

2. **Mix** the cheese with the herbs and stuff the peppers with the mixture.

3. **Pressing** the open ends together gently, dip the peppers into the beaten egg and then into the bread crumbs seasoned with salt and pepper.

4. **Add** the oil to a large heated pan and sauté the peppers until they are lightly browned on both sides.

5. **Remove** to a lightly greased casserole dish. The stuffed peppers can be made ahead to this point and refrigerated until ready for use.

6. **Bake** for 30 minutes.

Fried Green Tomatoes

Serves 4 to 6		
1½ cups	buttermilk, well shaken (see "Susie's Rules," page 263, for buttermilk substitute)	375 mL
2	large eggs	2
1½ cups	cornmeal	375 mL
1 tsp	kosher or coarse salt	5 mL
1 tsp	freshly ground pepper	5 mL
3	large green tomatoes (about 1½ lbs/750 g), cut into ½" (1 cm) thick slices	3
½ cup	vegetable oil	125 mL

1. **Whisk** together the buttermilk, eggs, 1 tablespoon (15 mL) of the cornmeal, ½ teaspoon (2 mL) of the salt, and ½ teaspoon (2 mL) of the pepper in a medium bowl.

2. **Dip** the tomato slices in the mixture.

3. **Heat** the oil over moderate heat until very hot in a heated 12" (30 cm) heavy skillet.

4. **Whisk** together the remaining cornmeal, salt, and pepper in a bowl.

5. **Dip** the tomato slices, one at a time, in the corn-meal mixture, shaking off the excess, and fry in the hot oil. The tomatoes should be golden brown and crisp on both sides.

6. **Drain** the tomatoes on paper towels and sprinkle with salt to taste.

Serve the tomato slices immediately

I know, I know. Not good for you, but sometimes you have to have a special treat. These are it.

Fabulous Frites

Serves 4		
4	large Yukon gold potatoes, peeled and sliced into 2" by ½" strips (5 cm by 1 cm)	4
6 cups	peanut oil	1.5 L
	Kosher or coarse salt to taste	

1. **Soak** the potatoes in ice water for half an hour.
2. **Drain** and dry well.
3. **Heat** the oil in a large, deep pot to 340 °F (170 °C). The potatoes are best cooked in batches in order to keep the heat of the oil to a consistent temperature.
4. **Add** a handful of potatoes to the hot oil and cook until light brown, about 2 minutes.
5. **Place** the potatoes on paper towels to drain and cool.
6. **Cook** the remaining potatoes in handfuls, always reheating oil to 340 °F (170 °C) before frying.
7. Once all the potatoes have been fried, **reheat** the oil to 375 °F (190 °C).
8. **Refry** the potatoes a handful at a time, until they are a deep golden brown, 2 to 3 minutes.
9. **Spread** on paper towels to drain.
10. **Sprinkle** with kosher or coarse salt and serve at once.

This is definitely not for anyone even thinking about cholesterol. If, however, you are like me and plan to die young and happy, try the kugel.

Potato Kugel

Serves 8		
¼ cup	rendered chicken fat	50 mL
5	medium potatoes, grated	5
1	large onion, grated	1
3	egg yolks, lightly beaten	3
1 tsp	kosher or coarse salt	5 mL
¼ tsp	freshly ground pepper	1 mL
¼ cup	all-purpose flour	50 mL
1 tsp	baking powder	5 mL
4	egg whites, at room temperature	4
3 Tbsp	chicken fat	45 mL

Preheat the oven to 375°F (190°C)

1. **Prepare** the chicken fat. (See "Susie's Rules," page 264, for rendering chicken fat.) Put the chicken fat in an 8" (20 cm) square baking dish, preferably one you can serve the kugel in.

2. **Place** the dish with the fat in the oven and heat until the fat is piping hot, about 5 minutes.

3. **Place** the grated potatoes and onion in a kitchen towel and squeeze out the excess water.

4. **Mix** the egg yolks with the salt, pepper, flour, and baking powder.

5. **Mix** the potatoes and onions with the egg mixture.

6. **Combine** and mix well.

7. **Whisk** the egg whites until they are stiff and hold a peak. Gently fold them into the potato mixture.

8. **Pour** the mixture into the hot pan and top with chicken fat.

Bake until brown, at least 1 hour and 15 minutes.

Pa's Buttery Mashed Potatoes

Serves 4

4	large Russet or Idaho potatoes, peeled and halved	4
1 Tbsp	kosher or coarse salt	15 mL
2 Tbsp	butter	25 mL
1 tsp	sour cream	5 mL
Dash	freshly ground pepper	Dash

1. **Soak** the potatoes in ice water for about 1 hour to ensure that they are nice and firm.

2. **Put** the potatoes in a large pot covered with cold water.

3. **Add** the salt to the water.

4. **Boil,** uncovered, for about 45 minutes. Test with a fork to ensure that they are cooked through. Drain.

5. **Put** the potatoes back into the pot and place on low heat in order to remove all excess moisture from the potatoes. Shake the pan so the potatoes don't stick.

6. When the potatoes are dried, **add** the butter and sour cream.

7. **Mash** vigorously to remove all the lumps.

8. **Taste** the potatoes. They may need more salt and certainly a dash of freshly ground pepper.

These are best made fresh, no matter what they say about pre-cooking. If you really must, you can pre-cook by making the pancakes till almost cooked through. Drain several times on paper towel until the towel is dry. Refrigerate until use. Then bake in very hot oven, 400°F (200°C), just till heated through. I am a purist when it comes to latkes, though, and do prefer them freshly made.

Grandma Jeanne's Potato Pancakes

Serves 4 for lunch or 8 as a side dish		
4	potatoes, peeled and grated (don't grate them too fine —it will make for a mushy pancake)	4
1	onion, grated	1
2	eggs, lightly beaten	2
2 Tbsp	all-purpose flour	25 mL
1 tsp	baking powder	5 mL
1 tsp	kosher or coarse salt	5 mL
½ tsp	freshly ground pepper	2 mL
1½ Tbsp	sour cream	20 mL
	Corn oil	

1. **Put** the grated potatoes in a towel and squeeze out the excess water.

2. **Mix** all the other ingredients, except the oil, together in a large bowl and add the potatoes.

3. **Heat** the oil in a large heated sauté pan or electric frying pan.

4. With a large spoon **add** the pancake mixture to the hot oil. I like my pancakes about 3" (8 cm) around, but you can make them any size your artistic sense demands.

5. **Brown** on both sides, turning once.

Serve hot with a dollop of sour cream or homemade applesauce (see page 240).

191

Fried Zucchini

Serves 4		
4	medium zucchini	4
	Kosher or coarse salt	
1 cup	all-purpose flour	250 mL
2 Tbsp	kosher or coarse salt	25 mL
1 tsp	freshly ground pepper	5 mL
2 cups	corn or olive oil	500 mL

1. **Wash** the zucchini and cut lengthwise into narrow strips about $1/4''$ by $1/4''$ (0.5 cm by 0.5 cm).

2. **Sprinkle** with salt and place in a colander. Drain for about 20 minutes.

3. **Rinse** well to remove all traces of the salt.

4. **Put** the zucchini into the seasoned flour in small batches and mix well. Remove from the flour, gently shaking to remove the excess flour.

5. **Heat** the oil to about 400°F (200°C) in a 12'' (30 cm) heated pan and fry the zucchini until it is golden and crisp.

6. **Drain** on paper towel.

Season with salt and pepper and serve.

Sweets

To know me is to know that I have an enlarged sweet tooth. And I mean sugar. The real thing, none of that chemical stuff. Maybe it will kill me, but I have no control over the need.

As I am finishing my main course, my thoughts go to dessert. I push my plate aside in anticipation of the sweet. Nothing wholesome, mind you, will do. The more decadent, the better.

None of the following recipes are elaborate. However, you do need a good mixing machine, the proper baking tools, good-quality baking chocolate, and time. See "Susie's Rules," page 263, for tips on great cake-baking.

Peach Upside-down Cake with Bourbon Sauce

Serves 8 with no leftovers

Topping:

½ cup	chopped pecans	125 mL
5	medium fresh peaches (about 1¾ lbs/875 g)	5
¼ cup	butter	50 mL
¾ cup	firmly packed dark brown sugar	75 mL

Cake batter:

1 cup	cake flour	250 mL
1 cup	all-purpose flour	250 mL
1 tsp	baking powder	5 mL
1 tsp	baking soda	5 mL
¼ tsp	salt	1 mL
½ cup	butter, at room temperature	125 mL
1 cup	granulated sugar	250 mL
1 tsp	pure vanilla extract	5 mL
⅛ tsp	almond extract	0.5 mL
2	large eggs, at room temperature	2
1 cup	well-shaken buttermilk (See "Susie's Rules," page 263, for substitutes)	250 mL

Accompaniments:

Bourbon sauce (see page 197)

Vanilla ice cream

Preheat the oven to 375°F (190°C)

For the topping:

1. **Put** the pecans on a foil-lined pan to roast. Put the timer on for 2 minutes and check every 2 minutes until the nuts are nicely roasted. Once you smell them, watch out—they're probably ready.

2. **Peel** peaches and cut in half. (See "Susie's Rules," page 265, for directions on peeling peaches.)

3. **Melt** the butter in a 10" (25 cm) cast-iron skillet over medium heat. Reduce the heat to low.

4. **Sprinkle** the brown sugar evenly onto the bottom of the skillet and heat, undisturbed, for 3 minutes (not all of the brown sugar will be melted).

5. **Remove** the skillet from the heat and arrange the peach halves close together, cut sides up, over the brown sugar. Sprinkle the pecans evenly over and around the peaches.

For the cake batter:

6. **Sift** together the flours, baking powder, baking soda, and salt into a bowl and set aside.

7. **Beat** together the butter and sugar with an electric mixer until light and fluffy and then add the pure vanilla extract and almond extract, mixing well.

8. **Add** the eggs, one at a time, beating well after each addition.

9. **Alternate adding** the flour mixture and the buttermilk a little at a time, slowly beating in each addition until just combined.

10. **Spoon** the batter over the mixture in the skillet, spreading evenly (be careful not to disturb the topping as the batter is quite thick).

11. **Bake** in the middle of the oven until golden brown and firm to the touch, 40 to 45 minutes. I have sometimes underbaked this cake because it is difficult to test—make sure that you insert a toothpick into the dough, not the peaches. The toothpick should come out dry.

12. **Remove** the cake from the oven to a wire rack and immediately run a thin knife around the edge of the skillet.

(continues on page 196)

13. **Invert** a plate over the skillet and invert the cake onto the plate (keeping the plate and skillet firmly pressed together). This is really a two-person job unless you have very strong hands. Carefully lift the skillet off the cake and replace any fruit that has stuck to the bottom of the skillet.

Serve the cake warm or at room temperature with hot Bourbon Sauce (page 197) and vanilla ice cream.

Bourbon Sauce

Serves 8		
½ cup	butter	125 mL
¾ cup	firmly packed brown sugar	75 mL
½ cup	heavy cream	125 mL
2 Tbsp	good bourbon	25 mL

1. **Melt** the butter in heavy medium skillet over medium heat.

2. **Add** the sugar and cook until a deep golden brown, whisking frequently, about 10 minutes. The mixture will be grainy.

3. **Slowly add** the cream and boil until the sauce is reduced, whisking occasionally, about 10 minutes.

4. **Test** for desired thickness by dropping ½ teaspoon (2 mL) of the sauce onto a plate and leaving to cool. This cool test will show you the thickness of the sauce. If you plan to reheat the sauce, you can undercook it a bit.

5. Just before removing the sauce from the heat, **add** the bourbon and cook for 1 minute.

The sauce will keep, covered, in the refrigerator for 5 days.

This is a quick and simple dessert when you are looking for something tart.

Pineapple Meringue Torte

Serves 8

Torte batter:

½ cup	butter, at room temperature	125 mL
½ cup	granulated sugar	125 mL
3	egg yolks, at room temperate (always separate the eggs when they are cold)	3
6 Tbsp	all-purpose flour	75 mL
1 tsp	baking powder	5 mL
¼ tsp	salt	1 mL
¼ cup	milk	50 mL

Meringue:

3	egg whites, at room temperature	3
Pinch	cream of tartar	Pinch
¾ cup	granulated sugar	75 mL
1 tsp	pure vanilla extract	5 mL
½ cup	chopped almonds	125 mL

Pineapple filling:

1 cup	drained crushed pineapple (8 oz/250 g)	250 mL
1 cup	heavy (35%) cream	250 mL
½ Tbsp	confectioner's (icing) sugar	8 mL

Preheat the oven to 350°F (180°C)

For the torte batter:

1. **Cream** the butter until fluffy and add the sugar 2 tablespoons (25 mL) at a time.

2. **Add** the yolks, one at a time, mixing well after each addition.

3. In a separate bowl, **mix** together 2 tablespoons (25 mL) of the flour and the baking powder.

4. **Alternate adding** the flour and milk, slowly beating in each addition until just combined. End with the flour and baking powder mixture.

For the meringue:

5. **Beat** the egg whites until light and frothy. I use a copper bowl for this process and a large clean whisk. You are most welcome to use an electric

machine, but you won't get as much volume as I do—your choice. Add the cream of tartar.

6. **Gradually beat** in the sugar and beat until the meringue is stiff and glossy.

7. **Add** the pure vanilla extract.

8. **Spread** the batter evenly in two 9″ (23 cm) ungreased round cake pans.

9. **Spread** the meringue on the top of the batter, ensuring that you go to the edge of the pan.

10. **Sprinkle** with the almonds.

11. **Bake** for 20 minutes.

12. **Cool** in the pans on a wire rack.

For the pineapple filling:

13. **Drain** the pineapple well.

14. **Whip** the cream until thick, slowly adding the icing sugar until well blended.

15. **Stir** in the well-drained pineapple by hand.

16. **Release** one of the cakes from the pan with an offset spatula and place on a serving plate, meringue side up.

17. **Fill** the torte with the pineapple and whipped cream mixture.

18. **Top** with the remaining layer.

19. **Refrigerate** for at least 3 hours. Remove from the refrigerator 30 minutes before serving.

My grandfather was a man of great taste. Uneducated, uncultured, but with innate good taste. And expensive taste. This expensive taste was passed on to my mom. She could recognize quality and she could recognize a bargain. Good tools.

Mother was brought up in a tenement, yet her father bought her a fox stole for her sixteenth birthday. I am not sure they even had enough to eat, but she had her stole. Beautiful things gave my grandfather and my mother such pleasure. She sure was acquisitive, but great fun to shop with.

There was a ladies' store in Brooklyn called Loehmann's. It was located in a rough section of town in a building that had been palatial in another era. There were two large marble lions guarding the entrance that I spent many an hour on as a little girl, waiting for Mom as she shopped.

The building was huge and crammed full of clothing. On the ground floor were the less expensive items. We would walk right on through. Never, never to stop there. Up the marble stairs to the "back room." Only movie stars, celebrities, and those with a special saleswoman were allowed in. The prices were high, but the clothes were to die for. In a moment, my mother could weed out the dregs and find just the right dress at just the right price. If there was only one that was outrageously priced, she'd nose it out in a sec. The woman had a real talent.

The place was filled with women only, in half undressed states of bra and slip. Remember slips? You would never go out of the house without a slip. I wonder what ever became of them. You would never go out of the house without your gloves, either. In the spring and summer we wore only white leather ones with little pearl buttons. Imagine trying to keep that clean.

Back to Loehmann's. You would grab your pile of clothes and find a spot to try them on. Someone was always yelling over, "Little girl, watch your purse." Things would have a way of getting misplaced there before you could turn around.

Mrs. Loehmann, the owner, would situate herself amongst this mass of bodies and watch us trying on her clothes. The bargains were truly great. My mother explained it thus:

"Susie, you see that woman over there?"

There she was, Mrs. Loehmann. White hair in a bun, a round, red rouge pat on each cheek, dressed in black (head to toe), and clutching a beat-up black purse.

"She does all the buying for the store. That purse is filled with money. She selects all these beautiful clothes at the factories and pays cash. The manufacturers don't have to wait to be paid and so she gets great discounts. That's how it's done!"

My first merchandising lesson from the master.

Shopping was an exhausting experience with my mother and so, after, as a treat, we would have dessert at a local luncheonette. Mother would have a cup of black coffee and a smoke and I would have chocolate cake and a cold glass of milk.

Me, at sixteen, with Mom outside the house in Brooklyn.

This is my tribute to the après-Loehmann chocolate cake, my Chocolate Cake to Die For. Don't even ask me where I got this recipe. I have had it so long, I take it as my own. It's a favorite of all my grandchildren, which makes it special to me—who should please them more than their grandmother?

This cake must be had with cold, cold milk. If you have it with soda pop or coffee, I will come back from my grave to haunt you.

Chocolate Cake to Die For

Serves 8

2½ oz	unsweetened chocolate (use the 1 oz/25 g squares)	65 g
⅔ cup	butter, at room temperature	150 mL
1¾ cup	granulated sugar	425 mL
2	eggs, at room temperature	2
1 tsp	pure vanilla extract	5 mL
2½ cups	sifted cake flour (I sift once, measure, and then resift)	625 mL
1¼ tsp	baking soda	6 mL
½ tsp	salt	2 mL
1¼ cups	ice water	300 mL

Preheat the oven to 350°F (180°C)

1. **Melt** the unsweetened chocolate over a double boiler while you are preparing the batter. Make sure the water level below is only 2″ (5 cm) and doesn't touch the upper boiler.

2. **Remove** the melted chocolate from the heat and cool slightly before adding to the batter.

3. In a large bowl, **thoroughly cream** the butter until it is quite fluffy. I recommend a look at "Susie's Rules," page 263, to review the basic rules of cake-making.

4. **Very slowly** add the sugar, beating well after each addition. I do this in ¼ to ⅓ cup (50 to 75 mL) additions; takes about 15 minutes.

5. **Add** the eggs one at a time, beating well after each addition. Always break the eggs into a small bowl and then add them to your baking mixture. This helps to prevent the possibility of adding a rotten egg that would spoil all your hard work.

6. **Add** the pure vanilla extract with the last egg.

7. **Add** the cooled chocolate to the butter, sugar, and egg mixture.

8. In a medium bowl, **sift** together the cake flour, baking soda, and salt.

9. **Add** the flour mixture (about ½ cup/125 mL at a time) to the batter, alternating with the ice water

(about $^{1}/4$ cup/50 mL at a time). Do this at a slow speed, beating just until the flour disappears and the water is slightly blended. Make sure that you do not overbeat the mixture. Do not leave for a phone call or a drink. Now it is important to work quickly!

10. **Pour** the batter evenly into two 9″ (23 cm) round cake pans lined with parchment paper.

11. **Bake** for 35 minutes and test with a skewer, which should come out dry.

12. **Slightly cool** the cakes in the pans on a wire rack. When they are cooled, carefully remove the paper.

Ice with Liz's Chocolate Frosting (page 204).

Liz's Chocolate Frosting

Makes or enough to ice a 9"(23 cm) cake		
1½ cups	heavy (35%) cream	375 mL
1½ cups	granulated sugar	375 mL
6 oz	unsweetened chocolate	170 g
⅔ cup	butter	175 mL
1½ tsp	pure vanilla extract	7 mL
Pinch	salt	Pinch

1. **Put** the cream and sugar in a medium saucepan and bring to a boil over moderately high heat.

2. **Reduce** the heat to low and simmer, stirring occasionally, until the liquid reduces slightly, about 8 to 10 minutes.

3. **Put** cold water and ice cubes in a large bowl and set aside.

4. **Pour** the mixture into a medium bowl and add the remaining ingredients.

5. **Stir** occasionally until the chocolate and butter are melted. Then set the bowl in the larger bowl of ice water.

6. **Beat** the frosting with a hand-held electric mixer on medium-high speed. Remember to scape the sides occasionally with a rubber spatula.

7. When the sauce becomes thick and glossy, about 5 minutes, **stop beating.** Pull the beaters up and see if the frosting is the thickness of a meringue. You must use at once, as it will thicken as it sits.

See "Susie's Rules," page 264, for icing tips.

Black and White Cupcakes

About 12 cupcakes

Batter:

½ cup	butter, at room temperature	125 mL
2	eggs	2
1 tsp	pure vanilla extract	5 mL
1¾ cups	sifted cake flour	425 mL
1 cup	granulated sugar	250 mL
½ tsp	salt	2 mL
1¾ tsp	baking powder	8 mL
½ cup	milk	125 mL

Filling:

1	egg yolk, beaten	1
⅓ cup	milk	75 mL
1½ tsp	good-quality instant coffee	7 mL
1½ tsp	cornstarch	7 mL
⅓ cup	chocolate chips	75 mL

Preheat the oven to 375°F (190°C)

For the batter:

1. **Cream** the butter, about 10 to 15 minutes.

2. **Add** the eggs and pure vanilla extract.

3. **Resift** the flour with the sugar, salt, and baking powder.

4. **Add** the flour mixture, alternating with the milk, to make about four additions of each. Do this with the electric mixer at a slow speed, beating just until the flour disappears and the milk is slightly blended. Remember to work very quickly once the flour has been added. Do not overbeat.

For the filling:

5. **Add** the beaten egg yolk to the milk in the top of a double boiler.

6. **Make** a paste of the coffee and cornstarch mixed with a little water.

7. **Add** to the milk mixture.

8. **Cook** until thick, stirring continuously.

9. **Add** the chocolate chips to the hot mixture.

10. **Set** cupcake papers in 2″ (5 cm) muffin tins.

(continues on page 206)

11. **Divide** the batter evenly among the 12 holders, using about $^1/_3$ cup (75 mL) per liner. Fill each of the liners halfway and then add the filling. Fill with the remaining batter.

12. **Bake,** rotating the pan once, until just golden and the tops spring back to your touch, about 20 to 25 minutes.

13. **Cool** on a wire rack.

Top with Whipped Chocolate Icing.

Whipped Chocolate Icing
(great for cupcakes)

Yield for 12 cupcakes		
3 oz	unsweetened chocolate	75 g
¼ cup	butter	50 mL
1 cup	confectioner's (icing) sugar	250 mL
1	egg	1
1½ Tbsp	hot water	20 mL
¼ tsp	pure vanilla extract	1 mL

1. **Melt** the chocolate and butter in a double boiler over simmering water. Cool slightly.

2. **Place** all the remaining ingredients in a small bowl.

3. **Beat** briefly with a hand-held electric mixer or whisk to just mix.

4. **Set** the bowl in larger bowl that has been filled about 3/4 full with ice.

5. **Add** the melted chocolate and butter and beat until the mixture thickens to the consistency of mayonnaise. Make sure it is thick enough that it won't run off the cupcakes. Remove from the ice water.

6. **Take** a cooled cupcake in your hand and dip and swirl it quickly in the icing. You need to work quickly or the icing will get too firm.

7. **Place** on a rack to set.

Every year, for my birthday, my mom and dad would take me to a show in the city (that's Broadway, kid) and then out for dinner at Lindy's. I loved the excitement of the theater. It smelled and looked different than anything I had ever known. Old velvet chairs, gilt paint, cigarette smoke (yes, we did smoke a lot then), and perfume.

I was taken mostly to musicals. Olsen and Johnson were a favorite of Grandma and Grandpa's. This is a long, long time ago, so most of you won't know Olsen and Johnson, but let me tell you, they could make you laugh. A lot!

I rarely got birthday presents. My mom, Grandma Jeanne, would say that every day was my birthday. Ever hopeful, I longed for a beautiful doll with hair. If I did get a gift, it was a Magic Skin Baby Doll, which was a treat the first time I received it, but after four or five birthdays, it was old hat.

Grandpa George once braved the truth by suggesting to Grandma, "Jeanne, maybe the kid [that's me] wants another kind of doll. "

You should be glad you weren't there for her response. Trouble lay ahead.

"Don't be silly," she said. "You don't want another kind of doll, do you, Susie?" she asked, incredulously.

What was I to do? Any answer other than "No, I don't" was worth two or three days of silence and anger from my mother. So it was Magic Skin Baby Doll for me. I learned in the trenches and wasn't about to make a mistake.

Back to Lindy's. Grandpa always did buy me a gift for my birthday. A live turtle with the map of New York on its back. Grandpa would hold the turtle in his fedora on his lap during the play and throughout dinner. The turtles, though well looked after by me, tended to live about a year, so a new turtle was required every year.

After the play, we would go to Lindy's. Long, long, long lines in the cold (February is my month) to finally be seated in a noisy dining room favored by the theatre and movie crowds. If you want to know more about Lindy's, just see *Guys and Dolls*.

The rudest, richest waiters in all of New York served at Lindy's. Chicken in the Pot was a family favorite. Then came the pièce de resistance—Lindy's renowned cheesecake. Creamy and light and, oh, so delicious.

The lesson is to always read recipes. Grandma found this one in a newspaper at least fifty years ago. She swore it was better than Lindy's.

Cheesecake

Serves 10

Crust:

4 oz	zwieback (baby cookies)	125 g
3 Tbsp	granulated sugar	45 mL
3 Tbsp	melted butter	45 mL

Cake:

1 lb	cream cheese, at room temperature	500 g
3 Tbsp	all-purpose flour	45 mL
1½ cups + 3 Tbsp	granulated sugar	375 mL + 45 mL
½ tsp	salt	2 mL
6	eggs, separated and brought to room temperature (always separate your eggs when they are cold)	6
1 tsp	pure vanilla extract	5 mL
1 cup	sour cream	250 mL

Preheat the oven to 325°F (160°C)

For the crust:

1. **Place** the zwieback in a food processor in small batches and make very fine crumbs.

2. **Mix** together the zwieback, sugar, and melted butter in a bowl. Set aside ¼ cup (50 mL) of this mixture for the topping.

3. **Heavily butter** a 10" (25 cm) springform pan.

4. **Press** the zwieback mixture around the sides of the pan and sprinkle a bit onto the bottom of the pan, ensuring there are not too many crumbs in the corners.

For the cake:

5. **Cream** the cream cheese until it is fluffy.

6. **Sift** together the flour, the 1½ cups (375 mL) of sugar, and salt.

7. **Slowly add** the flour mixture to the cheese. Mix well.

8. **Add** the six egg yolks, one at a time, beating well after each addition.

9. **Mix** the pure vanilla extract into the sour cream and add to the mixture.

10. Because the batter is quite heavy, make sure that you use your rubber spatula frequently to stir up the batter at the bottom of the bowl.

11. **Beat** the six egg whites in a separate bowl until stiff, slowly adding the 3 tablespoons (45 mL) of sugar.

12. **Fold** about 1 cup (250 mL) of the cheese mixture into the egg whites.

13. Then **fold** this mixture gently into the cheese.

14. **Pour** into the prepared pan and sprinkle with the 1/4 cup (50 mL) of topping.

15. **Bake** for 1 hour.

16. **Turn off** the heat but leave the cake in the oven for an additional hour with the oven door open.

17. **Cool** on a wire rack and refrigerate.

18. **Bring** to room temperature before serving.

This is one of the recipes my mom found just by reading the food column in her local paper, long before there were cooking magazines or the wealth of cookbooks that we have at our fingertips today. There is a special talent involved in reading recipes and knowing they will be delicious. Try this one, for sure!

Grandma Jeanne's Pound Cake

Serves 8

¼ lb	butter, at room temperature	125 g
3 oz	cream cheese, at room temperature	75 g
1 cup	granulated sugar	250 mL
2	egg yolks, at room temperature (always separate your eggs when they are cold)	2
½ tsp	lemon extract	2 mL
½ cup	milk	125 mL
1½ cups	self-raising flour, sifted	375 mL

Optional topping:

1 cup	chopped pecans	250 mL
¼ cup	brown sugar	50 mL

Preheat the oven to 350°F (180°C)

1. **Butter** well an 9" × 5" (2 L) loaf pan and sprinkle with about ¹/4 cup (50 mL) flour. Shake the pan about to ensure that the flour has covered it well and then toss out any remaining bits of loose flour. Set the pan aside.

2. If using the pecan topping, **put** the chopped pecans on a foil-lined pan to roast. Put the timer on for 2 minutes and check every 2 minutes until they are nicely roasted. Once you smell them, watch out—they're probably ready. Set aside to cool.

3. **Beat** together the butter and cream cheese until light and fluffy.

4. **Slowly add** the sugar until well combined.

5. **Add** the egg yolks one at a time, beating well after each addition.

6. **Combine** the lemon extract with the milk.

7. Alternately **add** the flour and milk a little at a time, slowly beating in each addition until just combined.

8. **Beat** the egg whites till meringue consistency and gently fold them into the batter.

9. **Pour** the batter into the prepared loaf pan.

10. If desired, you can now **add** chopped pecans mixed with brown sugar for a topping.

11. **Bake** for 55 minutes.

12. **Remove** from the pan to cool on a rack.

Marble Pound Cake

Prepare the dough for Grandma Jeanne's Pound Cake (page 210) and set aside.

Filling:

1½ tsp	good-quality instant coffee	7 mL
1½ tsp	cornstarch	7 mL
1	egg yolk	1
⅓ cup	milk	75 mL
⅓ cup	chocolate chips	75 mL

Preheat the oven to 350°F (180°C)

1. **Mix** the coffee and cornstarch together and make a paste by adding water a tablespoon at a time till you reach the consistency of a thick paste.

2. **Mix** together the egg yolk and milk and heat on the top of a double boiler over boiling water, medium heat.

3. **Add** the coffee paste, slowly stirring to ensure that no lumps form. Cook until slightly thickened.

4. **Remove** from the heat, add the chocolate chips, and stir till melted. Cool slightly.

5. **Pour** half of the pound cake batter into a well-greased and floured 9" × 5" (2 L) loaf pan. Add the chocolate mixture and then the remaining batter. With a spatula, cut through the batter to create a marble effect.

6. **Bake** for 55 minutes.

I bake my pies, especially the fruit ones, on a pastry saver or a baking sheet that has been lined with a silpat pad or parchment paper. Keeps the oven cleaner! I also wrap the edges of the crust with foil so that they don't brown too much.

I always make my Apple Pie Syrup (the recipe is included here) to ensure the pie juices thicken a bit.

Apple Pie

Serves 8, but with no leftovers or seconds

2	pastry rounds (see Can't-Mess-Up Perfect Pie Pastry, page 218), rolled out to 12″ (30 cm)	2
4 lbs	crisp, crunchy apples such as Granny Smith, Spy, or Cortland, cored, peeled, and quartered (save the peels and cores)	2 kg
3 Tbsp	all-purpose flour	45 mL
¾ cup	granulated sugar	175 mL
½ tsp	ground cinnamon	2 mL
Teeny pinch	ground nutmeg	Teeny pinch
½ tsp	salt	2 mL
3 Tbsp	cold butter, cut into small pieces	45 mL

Preheat the oven to 400°F (200°C)

1. **Fit** one of the pastry rounds into a 9″ (23 cm) pie plate and chill for at least 30 minutes.

2. **Place** the second round on waxed paper and refrigerate for 30 minutes.

3. **Slice** the apples into ¹/₂″ (1 cm) slices. If you slice them too thin, the pie filling will be mushy.

4. **Put** the apples into a large bowl and add the flour, ²/₃ cup (150 mL) of the sugar, cinnamon, nutmeg, and salt.

5. **Gently shake** the bowl in a tossing motion to mix well. Using a spoon will bruise the apples.

6. **Transfer** the apples and their juice to the pastry shell.

7. **Distribute** the butter over the apples.

8. **Cut** decorative vents into the top crust pastry to let the steam escape and then lay the dough over the fruit.

9. **Trim** the edges of the dough about 1″ (2.5 cm) over the pie pan, and seal and crimp the edges.

10. **Chill** the pie for about 30 minutes.

11. **Place** the pie on a silpat- or parchment-lined cookie sheet, as the juice will often escape. Cover the crust edges with strips of aluminum foil to prevent them from burning. Remove the foil after 12 to 15 minutes.

12. **Bake** the pie for about 1 hour, or until the crust is golden, and remove from the oven to cool.

Apple Pie Syrup:

13. While the pie is baking, **place** the apple peels and cores in a small saucepan and cover with water.

14. **Add** the remaining 2 tablespoons (25 mL) sugar, place over low heat, and simmer uncovered for 30 minutes.

15. **Strain** the syrup, which now has the flavor from just under the apple peel. If you use red apples, the syrup will have a rose color.

16. **Pour** 2 to 3 tablespoons (25 to 45 mL) of the syrup through the hole in the top of the pie as it cools and tip the pie gently from side to side to distribute the syrup evenly. You may want to add more syrup, as it is full of pectin.

17. **Let** the pie rest for another 45 minutes.

Best served with a scoop of vanilla ice cream atop a slice of warm pie.

This pie is only good during strawberry season. It's a pity that it's so seasonal, but it gives us something to look forward to. Seasonal fruits work best in their seasons. Being a purist, I don't freeze strawberries. I find they get water-logged when they defrost. Enjoy the moment.

Luscious Strawberry-Rhubarb Pie

Serves 6 to 8 with no leftovers

1	9" (23 cm) unbaked pastry shell (see Can't-Mess-Up Perfect Pie Pastry, page 218)	1
1	9" (23 cm) unbaked pastry top for lattice or decorative pieces	1
2 lbs	ripe strawberries, washed, hulled, and sliced	1 kg
1½ lbs	rhubarb, sliced into 1" (2.5 cm) long pieces	750 g
1 cup	granulated sugar	250 mL
¼ cup	cornstarch	50 mL
⅛ tsp	salt	0.5 mL
2 Tbsp	butter	25 mL

Preheat the oven to 400°F (200°C)

1. **Put** the berries and rhubarb into a large bowl.

2. **Combine** the sugar, cornstarch, and salt and stir into the berries and rhubarb by tossing the bowl several times.

3. **Fill** a prepared, unbaked pastry crust with the berry mixture and dot with the butter.

4. **Top** the pie with lattice or decorative piecrust pieces. Cover the crust edges with strips of aluminum foil to prevent them from burning. Remove the foil after 12 to 15 minutes.

I bake my pies, especially the fruit ones, on a pastry saver, a silpat- or parchment-lined baking sheet. Keeps the oven cleaner!

5. **Bake** in a preheated oven for 15 minutes.

6. **Reduce** the heat to 375°F (190°C) and bake for another 25 minutes or until the filling is bubbly and thick and the crust is browned. Cool on a rack.

Serve with whipped cream.

In the middle of the summer I wait patiently for fresh, preferably wild, blueberries. You can, however, make this pie with dry frozen (that is, without liquid) blueberries. The way to do it is to put the fresh washed and dried berries in the freezer on a tray until they are frozen. Then put them in an airtight plastic bag. Voilà! Fresh blueberries in December.

Blueberry Pie

Serves 6 to 8

1	9" (23 cm) unbaked pastry shell (see Can't-Mess-Up Perfect Pie Pastry, page 218)	1
1	9" (23 cm) unbaked pastry top for lattice or decorative pieces	1

Filling for 1 pie (can be doubled for 2):

4 cups	fresh wild blueberries	1 L
¼ cup	all-purpose flour	50 mL
1⅓ cups	granulated sugar	325 mL
½ tsp	salt	2 mL
2 Tbsp	fresh lemon juice	25 mL
1 cup	firmly packed brown sugar	250 mL
3 Tbsp	butter	45 mL

Preheat the over to 425°F (220°C)

1. **Wash** the blueberries, drain well, and put them into a large bowl.

2. **Combine** the flour, granulated sugar, and salt.

3. **Pour** this mixture over the berries and gently shake the bowl in a tossing motion to combine well. Using a spoon will only bruise the berries.

4. **Sprinkle** with the lemon juice and let stand for 5 minutes.

5. **Turn** the berry filling into the pastry shell, sprinkle with the brown sugar, and dot with butter.

6. You can **use** a top crust over the berries, cutting slits to allow the steam to escape. Or you can cut out pastry designs from the crust and place them over the berries. Cover the crust edges with strips of aluminum foil to prevent them from burning.

7. **Bake** the pie on a silpat- or parchment-lined cookie sheet, as the juice will often escape.

8. **Bake** until the crust is nicely browned, 40 to 50 minutes. Cool on a wire rack.

Lemon Meringue Pie

Serves 6 to 8 without a chance of any leftovers

1	baked 9" (23 cm) pastry shell (see Can't-Mess-Up Perfect Pie Pastry, page 218)	1
1 cup	granulated sugar	250 mL
¼ tsp	salt	1 mL
¼ cup	all-purpose flour	50 mL
3 Tbsp	cornstarch	45 mL
2 cups	water	500 mL
3	eggs yolks, at room temperature (It's easiest to separate the eggs when they are cold)	3
1 Tbsp	butter	15 mL
	Grated zest of 1 lemon	
¼ cup	fresh lemon juice	50 mL
	Meringue Pie Topping (see page 217)	

1. **Combine** the sugar, salt, flour, and cornstarch in a medium saucepan and stir in the water, ensuring there are no lumps.

2. **Cook** over low to medium heat, stirring constantly, until thickened and smooth. Do not leave to answer the phone.

3. **Stir** 3 tablespoons of the hot mixture into the beaten egg yolks. This will prevent the eggs from scrambling.

4. **Add** the egg yolk mixture to the pot, stir to combine, and cook, stirring, over a low heat for about 2 minutes.

5. **Stir** in the butter, lemon zest, and lemon juice and cool slightly in a bowl. Press plastic wrap onto the mixture to prevent a skin from forming while it is cooling.

6. **When** cooled, pour into the pastry shell.

7. **Top** with meringue (recipe follows) and brown in the oven as directed.

Meringue Pie Topping

Topping for a 9" (23 cm) pie		
5	egg whites, at room temperature	5
¼ tsp	cream of tartar	1 mL
½ cup	granulated sugar	125 mL
1 Tbsp	cornstarch	15 mL
⅓ cup	water	75 mL

Preheat the oven to 425°F (220°C)

1. **Beat** the egg whites until light and frothy. I use a copper bowl for this process and a large whisk. You can use the electric mixer if you prefer, but I'll get more volume my way.

2. **Add** the cream of tartar.

3. **Gradually add** the sugar and beat until the meringue is stiff and glossy. This will take a while, so don't rush it.

4. **Dissolve** the cornstarch in the water and heat in a small saucepan until a thick paste forms.

5. **Add** the paste to the meringue a teaspoon (5 mL) at a time so the heat does not disturb the meringue.

6. **Pile** the meringue onto the cooled lemon-filled pie, spreading it until it touches the edges of the pastry to prevent shrinking. Make any design you wish with the meringue, using a spatula or knife.

7. **Bake** until the top is brown, about 5 to 6 minutes. Watch closely!

8. **Cool** for at least 4 hours to set before serving.

Can't-Mess-Up Perfect Pie Pastry

2 crusts (9"/23 cm) or 12 medium tart shells		
2½ cups	all-purpose flour	625 mL
½ tsp	salt	2 mL
1 tsp	granulated sugar	5 mL
1 cup	frozen butter, cut into 16 pieces	250 mL
¼ cup	frozen shortening, cut in half	50 mL
½–¾ cup	iced water (bear in mind that in the summer, in a warm room, you will use less water than on a cold winter day)	125–175 mL

1. **Refrigerate** the flour, salt, and sugar in the bowl of the food processor until they are quite cold, about 20 minutes.

2. **Process** a moment to sift and then add the butter and shortening.

3. **Turn** the machine on and off quickly a few seconds at a time four or five times, or until the mixture begins to look like coarse meal.

4. **Add** the water in a slow stream through the feed tube while the machine is running.

5. **Process** just until the dough begins to gather around the blades, about 15 to 20 seconds. To check if the dough is done, grasp a small handful and if it holds together, it's done.

6. **Empty** the processor onto plastic wrap and press the dough into a ball. I use the wrap to push the dough together. You don't want the warmth of your hands to melt the butter or shortening, so work quickly.

7. **Divide** the dough into two equal pieces, flatten the pieces into two rounds, and wrap each piece in plastic wrap. Each piece of dough should look like a large, thick hamburger patty.

8. **Chill** in the refrigerator for at least 1 hour (or in the freezer for 20 minutes). The dough may be stored in the refrigerator for 3 to 4 days. Allow the dough to stand for a few minutes to soften slightly so that it will be easier to roll. Can be frozen for up to 6 months.

9. **Roll** the dough out onto a lightly floured board. Roll in all directions, turning the dough often. Make sure to keep the dough circular. If any cracks form, take a bit of dough from the edge, wet it with a dab of water, and paste it to the crack. After a few rolls, the crack or hole will disappear. Roll the dough about 1" (5 cm) larger than your pie plate, about $^1/_4$" (0.5 cm) thick. Remember, you have to work quickly to ensure that the small flecks of butter do not melt—they are what makes the crust flaky and perfect.

10. If baking a shell, **fold** the edges of the dough over the pie plate, flute to decorate, and pierce the dough with a fork in about ten places. I refrigerate it again so the dough can rest for about 30 minutes and the butter has a chance to re-harden.

11. If you are making a filled pie with a top, **fill** the pie plate with the bottom dough, and place the top rolled dough or decorations on wax or parchment paper and refrigerate for 30 minutes. Then fill the bottom crust, cut two or three holes in the top crust, place over the filled pie, and flute to decorate.

(continues on page 220)

For an unfilled pastry shell:

Preheat the oven to 375°F (190°C)

12. I **line** my shells with foil wrap that is weighed down with beans or stones to help to prevent the shell from shrinking. I also wrap the edges of the crust with foil as they have a tendency to cook more quickly than the shell.

13. **Bake** the shell for 12 to 15 minutes, checking the color of the crust edges. Then remove the weights and continue baking about 10 minutes more, until the entire shell becomes a lovely golden brown.

À Paris: Alan, Suzanne, Arthur, and me, eating and drinking as always, 2002.

French Apple Tarts

Makes 4 tarts

1	pastry round (I use store-bought puff pastry.)	1
	Egg wash, consisting of 1 egg yolk and ½ tsp (2 mL) cream	
4	baking apples	4
2 Tbsp	butter	25 mL
1 Tbsp	brown sugar	15 mL
4 tsp	butter	20 mL
¼ cup	vanilla sugar (see "Susie's Rules," page 267)	50 mL

Preheat the oven to 450°F (230°C)

1. **Roll** out pastry into a sheet and cut out four 6" (15 cm) circles. Then place the puff pastry on a baking sheet.

2. **Pierce** each circle about eight times.

3. **Braid** the remaining rolled dough to form a lip on each circle.

4. **Brush** the edge of the circle of dough with the egg wash and apply the braid. The dough can be refrigerated at this point until ready to use.

5. **Peel,** core, and thinly slice the apples.

6. **Sauté** the apples in butter in a nonstick pan until slightly browned.

7. **Sprinkle** with the brown sugar. Cool.

8. **Spread** the apple slices evenly in the center of each unbaked puff pastry.

9. **Dot** the tart with butter and sprinkle with some vanilla sugar.

10. **Refrigerate** until ready to bake.

11. **Bake** the tarts on a silpat- or parchment-lined cookie sheet, as the juice will often escape.

12. **Bake** until dough is browned, 15 to 20 minutes.

Serve warm with either vanilla ice cream or whipping cream and, for sure, Bourbon Sauce (page 197).

U se whatever plums are in season. Make the crust the day before the party and put the filling together just before baking.

Fresh Plum Tart

Makes a 9" (23 cm) tart

Crust:

6 Tbsp	butter, at room temperature	90 mL
¼ cup	granulated sugar	50 mL
3 Tbsp	almond paste	45 mL
1 cup	all-purpose flour	250 mL
2	large eggs, at room temperature	2

Filling:

1¾ lbs	Santa Rosa or prune plums, pitted, cut into ½" (1 cm) thick slices	875 g
½ cup	granulated sugar	125 mL
2 Tbsp	fresh lemon juice	25 mL
1½ Tbsp	cornstarch	8 mL

Preheat the oven to 375°F (190°C)

For the crust:

1. **Cream** the butter in an electric mixer until fluffy.
2. **Slowly add** the sugar until the mixture is creamy.
3. **Add** the almond paste until mixture is light and fluffy.
4. **Add** the flour and eggs and mix just until dough gathers together.
5. **Pat** the dough into the bottom and up the sides of a 9" (23 cm) tart pan. Refrigerate for 30 minutes.
6. I **line** my shells with foil wrap that is weighted down with beans or stones to help to prevent the shell from shrinking.
7. **Bake** for 12 to 15 minutes, checking the color of the crust's edges. Then remove the weights and continue baking until the entire shell becomes a lovely golden brown, about 10 minutes more.
8. **Transfer** to a rack to cool. This can be prepared a day ahead.

For the filling:

9. **Mix** the plums, sugar, lemon juice, and cornstarch in large bowl.

10. **Shake** the bowl to coat the plums with the sugar mixture.
11. **Place** the fruit into the baked shell.
12. **Cover** the edges of the tart with foil to prevent them from browning too quickly.
13. **Place** the tart on a baking sheet lined with a silpat pad or parchment paper and bake at 375°F (190°C) until the fruit is tender, about 30 minutes.
14. **Transfer** to rack and cool.

Four of my most favorite people—Sarah, Jess, Ruby, and Adam—my grandchildren.

Pear Tarts

Makes 4 tarts		
2	Bartlett pears, peeled and cored (try to leave the stem on for a pretty presentation)	2
3 cups	white wine	750 mL
1 Tbsp	ground cinnamon	15 mL
5 Tbsp	vanilla sugar (see "Susie's Rules," page 267)	75 mL
1	pastry round (I use store-bought puff pastry.)	1
	Egg white, beaten	1
2–3 Tbsp	melted butter	25–45 mL

1. **Place** the whole peeled pears in a saucepan with the wine, cinnamon, and 2 tablespoons (25 mL) of the vanilla sugar. Add water to cover.

2. **Cook** the pears until they're slightly tender to the fork touch. With a slotted spoon, gently remove the pears from the heat to cool slightly.

Preheat the oven to 400°F (200°C)

3. **Roll** out pastry into a sheet and cut out four 6" (15 cm) circles. Then place the puff pastry on a baking sheet. Pierce each circle about eight times.

4. **Braid** the remaining rolled dough to form a lip on each circle.

5. **Brush** the edge of the circle of dough with the egg white and apply the braid. Refrigerate until ready to use.

6. Leaving the stems on, **cut** the pears in half lengthwise. Thinly slice the pears.

7. **Place** the pear slices on the unbaked tart shells, creating a fan effect, and generously brush with melted butter.

8. **Sprinkle** with remaining vanilla sugar.

9. **Bake** on pan lined with a silpat pad or parchment paper until golden, about 15 minutes.

Serve with a warm caramel sauce (see page 238), ice cream, or whipped cream.

Ellen's Apricot Pastries

Makes 25 pastries

Pastry:

¼ lb	cold butter, cut into small cubes	125 g
½ cup	cottage cheese	125 mL
1 cup	all-purpose flour	250 mL
⅛ tsp	salt	0.5 mL

Apricot filling:

1 cup	dried apricots	250 mL
⅓ cup	granulated sugar	75 mL
½ cup	water	125 mL
1	egg white	1
½ cup	confectioner's (icing) sugar	125 mL

For the pastry:

1. **Put** the butter, cottage cheese, flour, and salt into the bowl of a food processor fitted with the steel knife.

2. **Process** until the dough forms a ball.

3. **Wrap** the dough in plastic, and refrigerate for at least 1 hour. (You can refrigerate the dough overnight or freeze it for up to 1 month.)

For the apricot filling:

4. **Put** the apricots, sugar, and water in a small saucepan and bring to a boil.

5. **Reduce** the heat to low and simmer, stirring occasionally, until the apricots are softened, about 8 minutes.

6. **Put** the apricots into a bowl and cut them into small pieces. If a knife doesn't work, scissors will. Set aside to cool. If the mixture is too thick to spread, you can stir in up to 2 teaspoons (10 mL) of water. You want the mixture to be the consistency of jam.

7. **Lightly beat** the egg white with a fork and set aside.

8. **Line** two baking sheets with silpat pads or parchment paper.

(continues on page 226)

9. **Roll** out the pastry dough on a lightly floured surface to a 10" by 10" (25 by 25 cm) square.

10. **Cut** the dough into twenty-five 2" (25 cm) squares.

11. **Spoon** 1 teaspoon (5 mL) of apricot filling onto the center of each square.

12. **Brush** the edges of the squares with the egg white.

13. **Bring** one corner of the dough to the center of the apricot filling. Fold the opposite corner of the dough to the center of the filling. Wet with the egg white and press lightly to seal.

14. **Transfer** the pastries to a baking sheet.

15. **Cover** and refrigerate pastries for at least 1 hour or overnight.

Preheat the oven to 350°F (180°C)

16. **Adjust** the oven rack to the middle of the oven.

17. **Bake** the pastries until they are golden, 25 to 30 minutes.

18. **Transfer** to a wire rack and cool.

19. **Sift** confectioner's sugar over the pastries. You can refrigerate them for up to 2 days or freeze them for up to 1 month.

If the pastries have been frozen, reheat in a 350°F (180°C) oven until warmed through, about 5 minutes. Serve at room temperature.

Karen's Butter Tarts

Makes 24 tarts

Pastry:

1 cup	frozen butter, cut in 1" (2.5 cm) cubes	250 mL
1½ cups	all-purpose flour, refrigerated for at least 1 hour	375 mL
½ cup	cold sour cream	125 mL

Filling:

½ cup	butter, at room temperature	125 mL
1½ cups	firmly packed brown sugar	375 mL
2	eggs	2
1 Tbsp	fresh lemon juice	15 mL
½ tsp	pure vanilla extract	2 mL
½ cup	raisins	125 mL

Preheat oven to 375°F (190°C)

1. **Process** the butter with the flour in a food processor fitted with the steel knife until it is the consistency of coarse meal.

2. **Add** the sour cream and process just until the dough forms a ball around the blades. Remember, never overprocess and scrape the bowl every now and then.

3. **Divide** the dough in two and wrap it in plastic wrap. Refrigerate for at least 1 hour or overnight. If you like, the dough may be frozen until ready to use, up to 6 months.

4. **Roll** out the dough and cut it into circles with a 2" (5 cm) cookie cutter or glass. Gently and lightly press each circle into an ungreased muffin tin to make 24 tarts.

5. **Mix** the butter with the brown sugar and eggs in an electric mixer until well creamed, about 1 minute.

6. **Add** the lemon juice and pure vanilla extract and beat until combined.

7. **Divide** the raisins evenly among the muffin shells.

8. **Fill** each cup about $2/3$ full with the creamed mixture.

9. **Bake** until golden brown, about 18 to 20 minutes.

10. **Cool** completely.

My husband, Arthur, and I used to holiday in Eleuthera in the Bahamas. Food came from the mainland—Miami—by boat and on "island time." No hurry, no rush, and, often, left out in the sun to turn rancid. There were no restaurants, no good grocery store, and no fresh fruit. Just ocean and beach.

Alan and Suzanne would often join us at this low-key, casual vacation spot, where the four of us cooked whatever we could get our hands on. It was dog eat dog at the dinner table. Chicken, chicken, and more chicken. Some fresh fish. Heavy, leaden, locally baked bread and no desserts.

However, by some miracle, we could get the ingredients for my mother's Choco-Nutto-Grahmo Cookies and they became a daily staple. Invariably, Suzanne would hide from us behind the open refrigerator door with just her tush sticking out as she gorged herself on the cookies. Deadly. It's impossible to have just one and more than one will likely kill you with calories and cholesterol. But they're real easy to make.

Susie, Suzanne, Alan, and Arthur carrying on in Eleuthera.

Grandma Jeanne's Choco-Nutto-Grahmo Cookies

Serves 8, unless Suzanne is there

½ cup	butter, melted	125 mL
1 cup	graham cracker crumbs	250 mL
1 cup	chopped pecans	250 mL
¾ cup	chocolate chips	175 mL
1	tin condensed milk (14 oz/398 mL)	1
1 cup	grated coconut	250 mL

Preheat the oven to 325°F (160°C)

1. **Layer** the ingredients in a well-buttered 8" (2 L) square baking pan in the order given, starting with the melted butter.

2. **Bake** for 35 minutes or until done. Test with a skewer, which should come out dry.

These easy-to-make brownies come to our kitchen from our friend Alan. I guess the very best thing about Alan is that he is a complete hedonist, just like me. At 9 in the morning he can think of shopping for those eats that you know you are going to want at 9 at night. Always planning and thinking ahead about food and treats. He is at once bright, interesting, handsome, stubborn, and great, great fun to be with.

Alan's Brownies

Makes 16 to 20 brownies

½ cup	margarine	125 mL
2 oz	unsweetened baking chocolate	50 g
2	eggs	2
1 cup	granulated sugar	250 mL
½ tsp	salt	2 mL
1 tsp	pure vanilla extract	5 mL
½ cup	all-purpose flour	125 mL
½ cup	chopped pecans	125 mL
½ cup	semi-sweet chocolate chips (I leave these out, but you might prefer to include them.)	125 mL

Preheat the oven to 350°F (180°C)

NOTE: It's important to mix the ingredients by hand so that a minimum of air is incorporated into the batter, thus making a rich, moist brownie.

1. **Slowly melt** the margarine and chocolate together in a double boiler over gently boiling water.

2. **Mix** together by hand in a bowl the eggs and slightly cooled chocolate mixture.

3. **Add** the sugar, salt, pure vanilla extract, and flour and blend well.

4. **Gently** fold the chopped nuts and chocolate chips into the batter.

5. **Pour** the batter into a lightly greased and floured 8″ (2 L) square baking pan.

6. **Bake** for 25 minutes. Check for doneness—a toothpick should come out moist.

These brownies are best when they are slightly under-cooked. Cut into squares.

Well now, Lundy's. There's a long story to be told here, but I will try to make it brief. It's about Sunday nights. Grandma Jeanne worked like a maniac all week long. When I think of all that she did in those days, I wonder how we working mothers ever dare to complain.

She was a whirling dervish in the kitchen and clean-up was always an unpleasant task for my mother, my maiden aunt who lived with us, and me. With the dishes came the arguments. Poor woman probably wanted to sit down with a smoke and stop for a minute.

So Sunday nights were the nights that we ATE OUT. Restaurant after restaurant. Sometimes with "the girls," her friends. Sometimes not. Chinese food, Italian food, and then there was Lundy's. It was at Sheepshead Bay and was reportedly the largest restaurant in the world (like that was a good recommendation), and it was always packed.

Head waiter? Don't be ridiculous. The first thing you did was split up. That way, the three or four or sometimes eight or ten of us would be able to increase the odds of finding a table. You'd carefully examine what course the diners were on. Were they inclined to eat quickly? Perhaps they were the most evil—those who knew you were waiting and deliberately dawdled (or was that my Brooklyn paranoia?). You'd stand and stare at them. Watching every mouthful and wishing them speed.

Others would try to take your table, much like a good parking spot, but you would fight them down. Grandma was the chief table-finder. Silly me, I lie, Grandma was The Chief! So now you are fighting for your life with people who are exactly like you, desperate for a table, and willing to do anything to get it.

First, however, Grandpa would take me to the bar for some clams and, undoubtedly, a scotch for him. Now comes the good part. The food. The first course ordered was always crabmeat or shrimp cocktail. Then the clam chowder—always ordered red by The Chief. Then the lobster. I don't think I was four when I had my first lobster. Young, eh? Mind you, The Chief sent me to sleep-away camp when I was four so why wouldn't she try to get me to

231

taste lobster? And she was right: the lobster was great. During all of this came hot, I mean, hot out of the oven, biscuits. Delectable! The butter would melt over them and drip down your chin as you forced mouthfuls in.

We were always told, "Don't fill up on the muffins, you'll have no room for supper." Who could listen to that? They were too good and well worth the "I told you so."

My son Andrew and his bride, Tova, at their wedding, November 2002.

Biscuits

Makes about 14 biscuits

1¾ cups	all-purpose flour	415 mL
1 Tbsp	baking powder	15 mL
1 Tbsp	granulated sugar	15 mL
½ tsp	salt	2 mL
4 Tbsp	unsalted butter	50 mL
4 Tbsp	shortening	50 mL
½ cup	whole milk	125 mL

Preheat the oven to 375°F (190°C)

1. **Sift** the flour, baking powder, sugar, and salt into a large bowl. Stir well.

2. **Cut** the butter and shortening into small pieces and add to the flour mixture.

3. **Using** a food processor, mix the butter and the shortening until the pieces are the size of a pea and the mixture resembles coarse cornmeal.

4. **Add** the milk and mix the dough just until it comes together. Be careful not to overmix.

5. **Roll** out the dough ¹/₂″(1 cm) thick. Not thicker and not thinner, if you want great biscuits. If they are too thin, the biscuits will be dry and over-cooked. If you roll them too thick, they won't cook properly.

6. **Using** a 2″ glass, cut out the biscuits and place them on an ungreased baking sheet.

7. **Roll** out the scraps and cut any additional biscuits.

8. **Bake** until the biscuits are golden brown, 14 to 15 minutes.

Serve hot with lots and lots of butter.

Ever the purist, I like my date-nut bread thinly sliced and served with cream cheese for a breakfast treat. This recipe is easy and delicious.

Liz's Date-Nut Bread

Serves 8

1 cup	coarsely chopped and pitted dates, preferably Medjool	250 mL
1½ tsp	baking soda	7 mL
3 Tbsp	butter, at room temperature	45 mL
¾ cup	boiling water	175 mL
1½ cups	all-purpose flour	375 mL
1 cup	granulated sugar	250 mL
½ tsp	salt	2 mL
1 tsp	pure vanilla extract	5 mL
2	eggs, beaten	2
¾ cup	coarsely chopped pecans	175 mL

Preheat the oven to 325°F (160°C)

1. **Butter** an 9″ × 5″ (20 cm × 10 cm) loaf pan.
2. **Toss** the dates with the baking soda in a medium bowl.
3. **Add** the butter and then pour the boiling water over the mixture. Let the mixture stand for 20 minutes.
4. **Whisk** the flour, sugar, and the salt in a large bowl.
5. **Add** the pure vanilla extract to the eggs and then add the egg mixture to the flour.
6. **Use** a fork to combine the ingredients. This takes a bit of work, as the mixture will be quite dry.
7. **Add** the dates and pecans.
8. **Stir** with a fork or wooden spoon until well blended.
9. **Pour** into the prepared loaf pan and bake for about 50 minutes, or until a toothpick tested in the center of the bread comes out clean. Remember when you are testing that the dates are moist and may fool you, so try several spots to ensure that you don't overbake the bread.
10. **Cool** in the pan for about 15 minutes and then turn out onto a rack to cool completely.

Serve for tea time or breakfast, thinly sliced and covered with cream cheese.

Apple Crisp

Serves 4		
1 cup	granulated sugar	250 mL
1 tsp	ground cinnamon	5 mL
6 cups	peeled, cored, and thinly sliced tart apples (about 5 large apples)	1.5 L
1 Tbsp	fresh lemon juice	15 mL
½ cup	all-purpose flour	125 mL
¼ cup	butter, cut into pieces	50 mL
1 cup	chopped lightly roasted pecans	250 mL

Preheat the oven to 350°F (180°)

1. **Butter** a 9″ (23 cm) round pie pan.

2. **Combine** ¹/2 cup (125 mL) of the sugar and the cinnamon in a large bowl.

3. **Add** the apples and lemon juice. Shaking the bowl will help to combine the apple and sugar.

4. **Transfer** to the pie pan.

5. **Combine** the flour and the remaining ¹/2 cup (125 mL) sugar in a medium bowl.

6. **Cut** in the butter until the mixture resembles fine meal. You can use a food processor, pastry cutter, or two knives for this step.

7. **Stir** in the pecans.

8. **Sprinkle** this praline topping over the apples.

9. **Bake** until the apples are tender and the topping is browned, about 50 minutes.

Serve warm with ice cream.

When I was a girl, a hurricane wreaked havoc on the tree-lined street where we lived in Brooklyn, so my father had to replace the grand old tree that had stood at the entrance to our home. Coincidentally, the Lehmans, our neighbors across the road, had to do the same.

Our house in Brooklyn, with the "baby" tree just visible on the right.

After he had watered the roses, tomatoes, and bleeding hearts in the back garden, Dad would come round to the front of the house to water the new tree. Tired at the end of his day's work, he would enlist me to be the tree waterer.

Did I come from a competitive world? Were these not truly upwardly mobile parents that I had? Were they not driven by some sort of neuroses to do better than anyone else? What do you think? My father had me out there watering that spindly little tree every spring and summer day that I was home so that our tree would grow "bigger than the Lehmans'." He would gauge my result daily, making sure that we won this battle in which we were the only participants.

"You see, Susie," he said, "we will have a grand tree and the Lehmans will not. An embarrassment, really."

Truth be told, years later, when I went back to the old neighborhood, guess who had the better tree? Only in Brooklyn would that matter to anyone.

Now I find that one of the great creative joys in my life is my own garden. For a little Jewish girl from Brooklyn to have trees (plural), tennis courts, a swimming pool—unheard of. But for this girl to grow her own vegetables, herbs, and, yes, even fruits, this was truly a gift from God. First of all, how could someone from an immigrant background own enough land for all of these things? What had the world come to?

So in my garden there grows rhubarb. Masses of it. For a few weeks in the spring, it becomes our dessert du jour.

I often cut this recipe in half and reduce the baking time.

Baked Fresh Rhubarb

Serves 8

2 lbs	rhubarb, cleaned and sliced about 1" (2.5 cm) thick	1 kg
1½ cups	granulated sugar, or to taste	375 mL

Preheat the oven to 400°F (200°C)

1. **Mix** the sugar with the rhubarb and put it into an ovenproof dish.

2. **Bake** the rhubarb for 15 minutes and then stir.

3. **Bake** for another 10 to 15 minutes. Check for doneness. Rhubarb should be soft.

4. **Check** frequently to avoid burning and remember that rhubarb has a tendency to boil over.

Serve warm with heavy cream.

Peaches in Caramel Sauce

Serves 2

½ cup	chopped pecans	125 mL
2	large, ripe freestone peaches	2
1 Tbsp	fresh lemon juice	15 mL
2 tsp	amaretto	10 mL
1 tsp	vanilla sugar (see "Susie's Rules," page 267)	5 mL
1 tsp	brown sugar	5 mL
	Butter	

Caramel Sauce:

½ cup	butter	125 mL
1¼ cups	granulated sugar	300 mL
2 cups	heavy (35%) cream	500 mL

Preheat the oven to 375°F (190°C)

1. **Put** the pecans on a foil-lined pan to roast.

2. **Put** the timer on for 2 minutes and check every following 2 minutes until they are nicely roasted. Once you smell them, watch out—they're probably ready.

Preheat the broiler

3. **Peel** and halve the peaches. (See "Susie's Rules," page 265, for directions on peeling peaches.) When you're ready to serve the dessert, place the skinned peaches, cut side up, on a baking sheet.

4. **Fill** the cavity of each peach with ½ teaspoon (2 mL) amaretto.

5. **Sprinkle** each peach with ¼ teaspoon (1 mL) vanilla sugar, ¼ teaspoon (1 mL) brown sugar, and a dot of butter.

6. **Place** under the broiler until nicely browned.

For the caramel sauce:

7. **Melt** the butter in a heavy medium skillet over medium heat.

8. **Add** the sugar and cook until a deep golden brown, whisking frequently, about 10 minutes. The mixture will be grainy.

9. **Slowly add** the cream and boil until the sauce is reduced, whisking occasionally, about 10 minutes.

10. **Test** for desired thickness by dropping ¹/₂ teaspoon (2 mL) of the sauce onto a plate and leaving to cool. This cool test will show you the thickness of the sauce. Cool slightly.

11. If you plan to reheat the sauce, you can **undercook** it a bit. The sauce will stay in the refrigerator, covered, for 5 days. Before serving, re-warm the sauce over medium heat, stirring frequently.

Serve the warm peaches topped with the roasted pecans, vanilla ice cream, and caramel sauce.

Even while dancing the night away with Arthur, I still have something to say.

Delicious on its own, smothered in thick whipping cream, or as a garnish for latkes (See Grandma Jeanne's Potato Pancakes, page 191). Really best when apples are in season.

Applesauce

Serves 8		
8	McIntosh apples	8
½–¾ cup	granulated sugar	125–175 mL

1. **Core** the apples and cut into quarters. Do not peel, as the red skin will nicely color the sauce.

2. **Put** the apples into a large saucepan and add about 1" (2.5 cm) of cold water.

3. **Add** ½ cup (125 mL) of the sugar.

4. **Cover** and bring to a simmer.

5. **Simmer** for 25 to 30 minutes.

6. **Taste** for sweetness. You may need to add more sugar, depending on the sweetness of the apples.

7. **Remove** the skins and put the apples through a food mill.

8. **Store** in the refrigerator, although the warm sauce with cold cream is divine.

After living in Toronto for three years, we finally moved from the boonies to "downtown." Downtown was Rosedale, at that time, an elegant old neighborhood of gracious houses with one new apartment building. That is where we lived.

In the early 1960s Rosedale was not home to people like us. We were surrounded by people who had never seen the likes of me before. First of all, I was Jewish. Then, and not the least of all, I was from New York. Brooklyn, actually. My clothes, my taste, my voice and its volume, my enthusiasm, my joie de vivre, my New York confidence (born of pushing onto the subway every day with doors closing you in so tight you had to learn to fold the newspaper to read it, praying all the time that some groping hands wouldn't find your derrière)—my very reasons for being were all too much for them to bear. Most were kind and interested. Some were dreadful.

My next-door neighbor in the apartment building was Jan Hyde-Smith. Who knew people with hyphenated names? I was used to Goldberg, Cohen, and Ginsberg. Jan was a southern Baptist, and her husband (the hyphen) was English. I mean real English. He was never comfortable with me. Thought I came from another planet. "Amusing creature, but keep her away from me!"

On the other hand, Jan was a big, open girl with a hearty laugh. A really decent woman. A stay-at-home mom (so was I, then) who baked bread, prepared hearty meals for her family of four, made her own Christmas decorations, sewed for her daughter, and cared for her family. Never a career girl. Always a wife and mother.

The point of the story is that I had never met anyone like her before. She was as odd to the little Jewish girl from Brooklyn as the girl was to her. We were two woman who had been brought up worlds apart. Me a New York–assertive, Jewish, career-girl mother and her an Oklahoman, Christian, stay-at-home mother.

Yet here we were—both loving mothers who tended to our families in the most nurturing of ways: we both loved to cook.

241

Jan's Lemon Chiffon Pudding

Serves 6

3 Tbsp	butter, at room temperature	45 mL
1 cup	granulated sugar	250 mL
3	eggs, separated, and brought to room temperature (it's easiest to separate the eggs when they are cold)	3
1 cup	milk	250 mL
¼ tsp	grated lemon zest	1 mL
¼ cup	fresh lemon juice	50 mL
⅓ cup	all-purpose flour	75 mL

Preheat the oven to 350°F (180°C)

1. **Cream** the butter well in an electric mixing machine until it's quite fluffy.

2. **Slowly add** the sugar to cream with the butter. This process should take from 10 to 15 minutes.

3. **Add** the egg yolks, combining well.

4. In a medium bowl, **combine** the milk with the lemon zest and lemon juice.

5. Alternately **fold** the flour and the milk mixture into the egg yolk mixture.

6. **Beat** the egg whites until stiff. Fold into the mixture.

7. **Spoon** the mixture into a well-greased, ovenproof 9″ (2.5 L) square baking dish. Set the dish in a *bain-marie* (a large pan filled with at least 1″/2.5 cm of water, into which you will put your baking dish).

8. **Bake** for 35 minutes or until done. Test with a skewer, which should come out dry.

Best served warm.

Watching TV in my youth meant watching wrestling and cowboys. I must have been about eleven when I decided to go horseback riding. Looked simple enough, and my friend Irma convinced me it was a piece of cake. I should have known I was in trouble when, dressed in my blue jeans, I met Irma at the subway and she was wearing jodhpurs and a helmet.

Off we went to the stable in Prospect Park, in Brooklyn. Irma easily hopped onto her horse and, when it was my turn, I explained to the stable hand that I had never ridden before.

"Bring out the old gray one," he yelled to someone back in the stable.

Out came the old, I mean really old, gray, miserable horse. With him came a stool for newcomers like myself. I climbed on and sat like a stone.

"What do I do now?"

"Listen, girlie," he said. "If you want to go right, pull the reins to the right. If you want to go left, pull the reins to the left. If you want to stop, pull both reins. Simple!"

And then he slapped the horse on his rump and off I went.

Our group of riders started off to the park. Irma hung back to help me navigate across the widest automobile circle in all of Brooklyn. Probably in the world, I thought. A circle with cars rushing to God knows where and none of them looking out for a girl on an old gray horse. It was terrifying.

Finally, we made it across and started our ride through the park. Everyone in the group trotted forward, but old gray and I hung back, walking slowly on the path, trying to get used to each other.

After a bit I started to get it. The feeling that man and horse are one. And so we slowly ambled on, until all at once, over a small rise, appeared a group of the dreaded "juvenile delinquents." These were the bad kids who could hurt you if they wanted to. In a group they were deadly. When they saw the horses, they picked up some rocks and started throwing them, shouting, "Let's get the gray one."

I quickly realize I am not astride white, or black, or chestnut. I am definitely on gray. The stones are hurled and my old, miserable gray horse is off.

Not walking anymore, oh no. Not even a mild trot for him. Running. Running like a crazy man, with me pulling on those reins. Left, pull. Right, pull. Both, pull. Nothing would stop the horse. I am yelling. I am screaming. I am really scared, but "old" horse turns out to be a good thing. Old means not much stamina, and so the horse finally stopped from exhaustion. And the kid from Brooklyn—me—I am still on top holding on to the reins, the saddle, whatever, but still on top.

At times like this, a girl needs some comfort. Nothing more comforting than some warm rice pudding topped with thick cream. Then you'd be ready to start a new day.

This rice pudding is the very best. The recipe has no cinnamon, but lots of raisins. Forget the diet and the cholesterol. Life is short. Enjoy the pudding.

Rice Pudding

Serves 6 to 8

3½ cups	milk	875 mL
½ tsp	salt	2 mL
¼ cup	long-grained white rice	50 mL
2	eggs	2
½ cup	granulated sugar	125 mL
½ tsp	pure vanilla extract	2 mL
½ cup	raisins	125 mL

Preheat the oven to 400°F (200°C)

1. **Rinse** a medium-sized saucepan with cold water and drain, but do not dry.

2. **Pour** in 2 cups (500 mL) of the milk.

3. **Add** the salt and bring to a boil. Watch the pot, as the milk has a tendency to boil over.

4. **Add** the rice, stirring for a moment or two until it is well mixed with the milk.

5. **Cover** the pot and let simmer over low heat until the rice is tender and the milk absorbed. This will take about 45 minutes, but be sure to keep your eye on it. Once again, watch that the milk doesn't boil over.

6. When the rice is soft and the milk is completely absorbed, **remove** the mixture to a bowl and set aside to let the rice cool to lukewarm.

7. **Mix** together well the eggs and sugar and add to the rice, along with the remaining 1 ¹/₂ cups (375 mL) of cold milk, and the pure vanilla extract and raisins.

8. **Wet** a 4-cup (1 L) casserole with cold water. Drain but do not dry.

9. **Set** the dish in a *bain-marie* (a large pan filled with at least 1″ (2.5 cm) water, into which you will put your baking dish). As this water warms, it will help to set the pudding.

10. **Spoon** the pudding into the casserole.

11. **Bake** until the pudding has a light brown crust on top. Test for doneness by inserting a skewer after it has been in the oven for 30 minutes. Don't let it get too dry. It firms as it cools. It seems to me that the pudding needs to bake for about 1 hour.

Serve warm or cold with thick cream.

Other Good Stuff

While this is a small section, it is the one filled with family recipes for jams and pickling and sweet drinks. Worth a look-see.

Bread Crumbs

Makes 3 cups (750 mL)

10–15 slices	bread (I use French bread or challah—egg bread), baked on a rack at 200°F (90°C) until dried out (Watch carefully to ensure the bread does not burn!)	10–15 slices

Seasoned bread crumbs:

3 cups	fresh bread crumbs	750 mL
4 Tbsp	dried oregano	50 mL
2 Tbsp	dried thyme	25 mL
2 Tbsp	dried basil	25 mL

To make bread crumbs:

1. **Place** the baked bread slices in a food processor and process well until the crumbs are the texture you prefer.

To make seasoned bread crumbs:

2. **Add** all the herbs and mix well.

Store the bread crumbs in a well-sealed plastic container in a cool, dry place. The bread crumbs will keep for one to two weeks but are best fresh.

Creamy Yummy Mayonnaise

Makes about 1 cup (250 mL)		
1	egg yolk	1
1	egg	1
2 Tbsp	fresh lemon juice or Herb Vinegar (see page 250)	25 mL
¾ tsp	Dijon mustard	3 mL
½ tsp	kosher or coarse salt	2 mL
¼ tsp	freshly ground pepper	1 mL
1½ cups	corn oil	375 mL

1. **Put** the egg yolk, egg, lemon juice or vinegar, mustard, salt, and pepper into the bowl of a blender and process until the mixture becomes creamy, about 15 seconds.

2. While the blender is running, **pour** in the oil very, very slowly in a thin stream until you reach the right consistency.

3. **Taste** for seasoning before storing, covered, in the refrigerator.

Mayonnaise will keep refrigerated for about 1 week.

Any type of tomato will do, but plum tomatoes are the best. Don't consider this recipe unless you are using summer tomatoes—there is no other kind.

Oven-Dried Tomatoes

Makes 2 large jars

10	plum tomatoes	10
1 Tbsp	kosher or coarse salt	15 mL
½ tsp	freshly ground pepper	2 mL
1 tsp	granulated sugar	5 mL
8 sprigs	fresh thyme, chopped	8 sprigs
¾ cup	chopped fresh oregano, including stems	175 mL
1 cup	chopped fresh basil	250 mL
½ cup	chopped Italian parsley	125 mL
2	garlic cloves	2
	Olive oil	

Preheat the oven to 200°F (90°C)

1. **Line** two baking sheets with parchment paper.

2. **Cut** the plum tomatoes in half and remove the seeds.

3. **Lay** the tomatoes on the baking sheets, cut sides up. Sprinkle with salt, pepper, sugar, thyme, oregano, basil, and parsley.

4. **Bake** until the juices have stopped running and the tomatoes are leathery, but not hard. This could take from 6 to 10 hours. Keep checking because the cooking time will vary.

5. **Put** one clove of garlic in each of two sterilized jars.

6. **Divide** the herbs and dried tomatoes between the two jars and submerge in olive oil. Cover and refrigerate.

The tomatoes will keep for up to 1 year. Use the oil for marinades, for Andy's Pasta with Divine Tomato Sauce (page 108), or for simply frying vegetables.

I get such pleasure going to my little herb garden and picking as I cook. I bury my nose in my hands and smell fresh. When the herbs are at their peak, I look forward to spending a morning with my vinegar.

Herb Vinegar

Makes 4 quarts (4 L)		
4 bottles	best-quality champagne or white wine vinegar	4 bottles
1 cup	fresh thyme	250 mL
1 cup	fresh oregano	250 mL
1/2 cup	tarragon	125 mL

1. **Heat** the vinegar to boiling in a large pot.

2. **Pack** the fresh and cleaned herbs into four 1-quart (1 L) sterilized glass jars until half-filled.

3. **Pour** the hot vinegar over the herbs. Seal and store in a dark place for 4 to 6 days.

4. **Place** a fresh sprig or two of the herbs in decorative bottles.

5. **Pour** the herb vinegar through cheesecloth to fill the glass bottles.

6. **Discard** the marinated herbs.

7. **Seal** the bottles and store in a cool dark place or refrigerate until needed, for up to one year.

8. When decanting, **add** fresh herbs to your decorative vinegar bottle.

This condiment is great with chicken, particularly Southern Fried (see page 166).

Pickled Watermelon Rind

Makes 2 pints (1 L)		
6 cups	peeled and diced watermelon rind	1.5 L
¼ cup	kosher or coarse salt	50 mL
2 cups	granulated sugar	500 mL
1½ cups	white vinegar	375 mL
1" piece	fresh ginger, thinly sliced	2.5 cm piece
6	whole cloves	6
2	cinnamon sticks	2

1. **Toss** the watermelon rind with the salt in a bowl. Cover and leave at room temperature for 6 hours or overnight.

2. **Rinse** the rind very well to remove the salt.

3. **Place** in a medium saucepan with enough cold water to cover.

4. **Bring** to a boil over high heat. Reduce the heat to low and simmer until tender, about 10 minutes.

5. **Drain** well.

6. **Combine** the sugar, vinegar, ginger, cloves, cinnamon sticks, and ½ cup (125 mL) water in another medium saucepan.

7. **Bring** to a boil, stirring to dissolve the sugar.

8. **Add** the watermelon rind and return to a boil. Reduce the heat to low and simmer, stirring occasionally, until the rind is translucent, about 15 minutes.

9. **Spoon** the rind and syrup into two 1-pint (500 mL) sterilized jars.

10. **Cover,** cool briefly, and refrigerate for up to 3 months.

When June comes, so do the strawberries and Arthur's annual ritual of making his delicious strawberry jam. The whole house smells of summer. Nothing better than taking a piece of white bread or challah and dipping it into the pot of cooking jam. Mouth-watering.

One June, when Arthur and I were first together, we were invited to a party at our friends', the Greens. The guests were people from my first life, and I was anxious that they admire my new man.

The day of the party was the day of Arthur's annual straw-berry orgy. He would be up at 6:00, cleaning berries. By noon, he would get into the white wine, which was needed to keep up his spirits, encourage his creativity, and keep him on his feet. I nagged at him most of the day, reminding him of our evening's commitment and my fervent desire that he impress the hell out of everyone at the party.

Arthur, just hanging out. He does that the best, and I love him dearly for it.

Many, many glasses of wine later, we began to dress for the party. I knew that I had lost Arthur for the evening when I opened the closet door and found him standing inside staring at his ties in wonderment. I was torn between wanting to kill him and laughing at the sight of him.

Arthur fell asleep in the car as I drove us to the party. When I woke him from his nap, he was grinning from ear to ear, but was clearly still not capable of holding an intelligent conversation. I explained to him that I was going to walk him into the party, sit him on a sofa, and stay by his side all night. Then I begged him not to say a word to anyone. Not a single word, lest they realize that he'd been into the sauce.

And so we sat on the sofa all night. People would come by to talk, but Arthur, good as his word, never said anything. Smiled and smiled and smiled. And you know what? Everyone thought he was charming. Thought he was soooo intelligent. They thought he had a great sense of humor. That's because all he did was sit there, listen, and smile. What a lesson!

Pa's Strawberry Jam

Makes 16 quarts (16 L), 30 to 36 8-oz (250 mL) jars		
32 lbs	fresh strawberries	16 kg
32 cups	granulated sugar	8 L

1. **Wash** the berries and remove the stems. Doing it this way helps to prevent the strawberries from becoming water-logged. Drain the berries.

2. **Place** the whole berries and the sugar into two large pots.

3. **Bring** to a boil over high heat. Reduce the heat to low and simmer, uncovered, skimming off the white foam as it rises to the top. Stir occasionally.

4. To test for the setting point, **keep lifting up** the spoon as you stir the jam. Initially, the pan liquid will run off the spoon at a great speed. As the setting point approaches, the stream will slow down and, eventually, two drops on each side of the spoon will come slowly together, forming a sheet that seems to hang and hesitate on the spoon. Your jam is now "set" and ready to jar. Don't overcook it, as the jam will thicken during sterilization.

5. **Fill** clean, sterilized jars almost to the top, leaving about ½" (1 cm), and put on the lids.

6. **Sterilize** the filled jars for 20 minutes in boiling water.

7. **Remove** to let stand and cool. Don't be disturbed when the lids start popping—it shows that they have sealed properly.

Store in a cool, dark place for up to 1 year.

Seville Orange Marmalade

Makes about 14 4 oz (125 mL) jars

2 lbs	Seville oranges (6 to 8 oranges, depending on size)	1 kg
6–7 cups	granulated sugar	1.5–1.75 L
	Water	

1. **Wash** the oranges in soapy water. Rinse well and remove the stem ends.

2. **Halve** and **juice** the oranges and strain the juice, reserving all the seeds and any loose membranes that have detached themselves from the skins.

3. **Slice** each orange peel into four sections so that you can remove the white pith.

4. **Thinly slice** the peels and combine with the juice.

5. **Measure** the mixture into a stockpot—there should be about 6 cups (1.5 L).

6. **Tie** the seeds and any membranes loosely in a double thickness of cheesecloth and add to the saucepan.

7. **Add** water to equal the volume of the peel and juice, plus 1 cup (250 mL). So to 6 cups (1.5 L) of peel and juice you will add 7 cups (1.75 L) of water.

8. **Bring** the mixture to a boil over high heat. Reduce the heat to low and simmer, uncovered, until the peel becomes translucent. This takes about 2 hours. Stir frequently, pressing the bag of seeds to help extract the thick juices that accumulate. You can cool this mixture, cover it, and refrigerate up to 3 days if you wish.

9. **Measure** the peel and water mixture into a large heavy pan. There should be 6 to 7 cups (1.5 to 1.75 L). Add water if necessary to get this volume.

10. **Add** an equal volume of sugar and, stirring constantly, bring to a boil over high heat, skimming off the foam.

11. **Boil**, stirring constantly, until the marmalade sets, 10 to 15 minutes. To test for the setting point, keep lifting up the spoon as you stir the marmalade. Initially, the pan liquid will run off the spoon at a great speed. As the setting point approaches, the stream will slow down and, eventually, two drops on each side of the spoon will come slowly together, forming a sheet that seems to hang and hesitate on the spoon. Your marmalade is now "set" and ready to jar. Don't overcook it because the marmalade will thicken further during sterilization.

12. **Fill** your clean, sterilized jars almost to the top, leaving about 1/2″ (1 cm), and put on the tops.

13. **Sterilize** the filled jars for 20 minutes in boiling water.

14. **Remove** to let stand and cool. Don't be disturbed when the lids start popping. It shows that they have sealed properly.

15. **Store** in a cool and dark place for up to 1 year.

Halina's Peach Jam

Makes about 16 ½-pint (250 mL) jars

6	eating oranges	6
	Peel of 2 lemons	
2 dozen	peaches	2 dozen
	Granulated sugar	

1. **Wash** the oranges and lemons before peeling. Use a vegetable peeler to remove the peels, then finely slice them.

2. **Remove** the white pith from the oranges, then quarter and finely chop them.

3. **Peel** and slice the peaches ½" (1 cm) thick. (See "Susie's Rules," page 265, for directions on peeling peaches.) Mix with the orange mixture and the peels.

4. **Weigh** the fruit and add sugar equal to that weight. Place these ingredients in a large pot.

5. **Simmer** for 2 hours. To test for the setting point, keep lifting up the spoon as you stir the jam. Initially, the pan liquid will run off the spoon at a great speed. As the setting point approaches, the stream will slow down and, eventually, two drops on each side of the spoon will come slowly together, forming a sheet that seems to hang and hesitate on the spoon. Your jam is now "set" and ready to jar. Don't overcook it, as the jam will thicken during sterilization.

6. **Fill** the clean, sterilized jars almost to the top, leaving about ½" (1 cm), and put on the lids.

7. **Sterilize** the filled jars for 20 minutes in boiling water.

8. **Remove** to let stand and cool. Don't be disturbed when the lids start popping—it shows that they have sealed properly.

Store in a cool, dark place for up to 1 year.

If you were brought up in Brooklyn in the 1940s by upwardly mobile Jewish parents, you went to camp for the summer. Sleep-away camp. Camp was to get you out of the hot city and into a healthy environment. I was sent at the age of four, which meant that my mother did not have to worry about what she was going to do with me for two months while she was at work.

Camp was in the Adirondack Mountains. The first summer I went, I remember always looking for my big brother, Larry, in a sea of "dreaded" boys. Whenever I did see him, he was covered in pink from the calamine lotion for the poison ivy he seemed always to be getting into. This is probably the first memory that I have of him. Pink!

Camp was the same every year. Purchasing the required clothes, blue for days and whites for Friday night suppers and religious services. Name tags sewn on every item so that you might, if you were lucky, come home with some of your own clothes. A canteen, a tennis racket, and you were ready to go. Year after year, one cabin to another, the ritual always the same. Rushing to find the least uncomfortable bed, putting your belongings into your "cubby hole" and making yourself as small as you could that first night at camp so that the spiders and other bugs wouldn't get you.

Camp was run like the army. There was clean-up every morning, scheduled meals, nap times, laundry days, and letter-writing hour; rigid, rigid, rules never to be broken. We were

At camp, with me between my brother, Larry, and his friend Eileen.

257

such good kids in those years that the rules never were broken. Do as you're told and remember the starving children in Europe!

One night a week there was a "social," where we giggling, awkward little girls would spend the evening dancing with giggling, awkward little boys. Oh, the terror of not knowing whether you would be picked to dance. Slow dance, that is. Bodies touching and pressing. Arousal for all. Our actions went no further than a kiss, which was then discussed and dissected by our cabin-mates well into the night. It was particularly interesting and disgusting if the boy in question wore braces. How on earth did we manage?

I loved camp. I was a good athlete and my competitive spirit thrived there. My first successes in life were at camp. I remember when my group all trouped off for tryouts for a camp play. *Cinderella,* it was. On our return from the auditions, the older campers yelled out, "Who got the part of Cinderella?" They were shocked to learn that it was me.

"But," they said, "Susie can't sing."

"You're right. But she was the only one we could hear at the back of the rec hall."

See—no talent, but a lot of chutzpah and very loud.

Being at camp also meant that I would get letters from my dad. These were the only times in my life when he would reach out to touch me. The letters were filled with humor and were sometimes read aloud to the whole camp for everyone's amusement. Often the letters accompanied a "care" package. Bubble gum, salami, and chocolates. Because, of course, the food at camp stank! I would go there skinny and come home emaciated.

The Lemonade and Malted Milkshake recipes that follow come from those times when I was so skinny that carbohydrates and sugar were words other people used. Oh, how I long for those days.

Lemonade

Makes about 4 cups (1 L)

Simple syrup:

²/₃ cup	water	150 mL
²/₃ cup	granulated sugar	150 mL

Lemonade:

²/₃ cup	fresh lemon juice	150 mL
2 cups	water	500 mL

For the simple syrup:

1. **Bring** the water and sugar to a boil in a small saucepan.

2. **Stir** and continue to boil until the sugar is completely dissolved.

3. **Cool** the syrup.

4. The syrup may be made 2 weeks ahead and refrigerated, covered.

For the lemonade:

5. **Put** the simple syrup in a pitcher.

6. **Add** the lemon juice and water.

7. **Combine** well.

8. **Refrigerate.**

When serving, pour the juice over a glass half-filled with ice.

Until my late forties, when I stopped smoking as a birthday gift for my husband, I was thin. That's an understatement—no curves and probably anorexic, an unknown condition then.

I was so thin as a child that one doctor recommended that I eat my dinner in bed to "retain" the food. I spent the spring that year looking out my window at my boy friends who were playing ball in the streets of Brooklyn without me. I was not only skinny, I was a real tomboy—boys and I were on equal footing so far as sports went.

The doctor's prescription didn't work. I not only didn't gain an ounce, I lost a spring season of stickball, stoopball, and a lot of Brooklyn fun.

I was encouraged to eat anything I wanted, which helps to explain my sweet tooth. I drank every malted, ate every chocolate and cake I could get my hands on. Didn't matter. Still skinny.

Malted Milkshakes

Makes 4 glasses		
2 cups	milk	500 mL
6 Tbsp	malted milk powder	90 mL
1 pint	chocolate ice cream	500 mL

1. **Place** the milk and malt powder in the jar of a blender and process until the malt is dissolved.

2. **Add** half the ice cream and blend until smooth.

3. **Add** the remaining ice cream until it is fully incorporated.

4. If the milkshake is too thick, simply **add** more milk.

Susie's Rules

I in this section, I've listed some of my own house rules for cooking: how to make a bouquet garni, clean leeks, peel peaches, and even make a pie crust. Life is full of rules, so here are some of mine.

Asparagus, preparation and storage

Keep your asparagus fresh from the market by standing them in 1″ (2.5 cm) water in a tall glass, then put them in the refrigerator. When they're ready to cook, cut or break off the bottom of each spear. Peel about 2″ (5 cm) of the bottom of the asparagus with a vegetable peeler. Soak in cold, salted water for a moment to clean. Steam or boil them until tender, about 3 to 5 minutes.

Basting chicken

I'm a little extra neurotic when it comes to basting. I don't tell too many people about this, but I'm prepared to share my shtick with you. I baste with the speed of a comet. I'm convinced that if I leave the oven door open for a leisurely baste, the chicken will get tough and the skin will uncrisp, after all my work.

Since my husband Arthur is usually the poultry baster in our house, I have a real worry. He approaches cooking with a much more easygoing and relaxed attitude than I do. Well, of course. He approaches everything with a much more easygoing and relaxed attitude than I do. So, I've convinced him to take the bird out of the oven, close the door, baste, and then

return the bird to the still-hot oven.

These are the things people who love each other do for each other.

Bouquet garni

1	bay leaf	1
6 sprigs	fresh parsley	6 sprigs
6 sprigs	fresh thyme	6 sprigs

Wrap them in cheesecloth and tie with kitchen string.

OR

6 sprigs	fresh parsley	6 sprigs
6 sprigs	fresh thyme	6 sprigs
1	bay leaf	1
1	celery stalk, cut in two	1

Put the parsley, thyme, and bay leaf in the hollow of one half of the celery. Cover with the other half and tie with kitchen string.

Brining chicken

Brining ensures a moister, better seasoned, and better caramelized chicken, in part because of the sugar in the brining liquid. I brine all my poultry before cooking. This recipe will brine a bird, whole or in pieces, up to 10 pounds (5 kg).

¾ cup	kosher salt or 6 Tbsp (60 mL) table salt	175 mL
¾ cup	sugar	175 mL
4 cups	water	**1 L**

Dissolve the sugar and salt in the water in a large zip-lock plastic bag. Add the chicken and seal the bag, pressing out as much air as possible. Refrigerate for 2 to 8 hours.

Remove the chicken from the brine and rinse well in order to remove all traces of the salt. Remember, *rinse well in order to remove all traces of salt.* No kidding around. You'd be surprised how the chicken retains the salt. Dry the chicken thoroughly.

For extra-crisp skin, let the chicken dry, uncovered, on a rack in the refrigerator for 8 to 24 hours. If you prefer not to brine, use a kosher chicken. It's already salted and has a taste and texture similar to a brined bird.

Butter

Always means unsalted butter. Always means room temperature for baking, unless otherwise noted.

Buttermilk, substitute

If you don't have any buttermilk, make a substitute with 1 tablespoon (15 mL) lemon juice or white vinegar plus enough whole milk to make 1 cup (250 mL). Let the mixture stand for 5 minutes before using.

Cake-making (universal rules for the cakes in this book)

Follow these rules and I promise you'll make a quality cake. A good electric mixer is a big help.

Almost all cakes, angel cakes not included, require the following plan of action. They all contain fat, eggs, flour, and a liquid, plus a host of other seasonings. Therefore:

1. **Whip** room temperature butter until real creamy. At least 10 minutes, 15 is better.

2. **Slowly add** the sugar and continue to beat for at least 10 to 15 minutes. If the phone rings, you can take the call and keep on whippin'.

3. Throughout the process, **stop** the machine and use a rubber spatula to stir up bottom.

4. **Break** the eggs into a small bowl one at a time to ensure that you don't add a rotten one to your batter. Then add them to the batter one at a time, beating well after each addition.

5. **Add** whatever other ingredients are called for, except the flour and liquid.

6. Now comes the trick. **Alternate adding** the flour and liquid in three to five steps. Beat the flour slowly and stop as soon as it is incorporated into the batter. The same goes for the liquid. Stop the moment it is slightly incorporated. Remember that most cakes fail because of overbeating the flour. No phone calls now. Utter concentration on the task at hand.

To render chicken fat (*schmaltz*)

Put ³/₄ pound (375 g) of chicken fat (easily purchased from a kosher butcher), one whole onion, and one thinly sliced onion into a saucepan. Cover and cook over low heat for 10 minutes. Remove the cover and brown the onions and skin left from the fat. This skin is called *grebenes*. You can easily kill someone with these fat-laden, beautifully browned pieces of onion and skin. I have to hide them from my husband, Arthur, who I really want to stick around for a while. Note: Store the unused fat in the refrigerator. Great to use when making Matzo Balls (see page 31).

To chiffonade herbs

Stack a clean leafy herb, like basil, in a little pile, then roll up the leaves to cigarette size. Slice across the bundle. Use at once, as the basil will discolor.

Garlic

Always cut the clove in half and remove the inner green core. By adding the garlic to *room-temperature oil* when cooking, you prevent the garlic from burning.

Ginger

You can keep well-wrapped fresh ginger in the freezer and grate it as required.

Icing and frosting cakes

Place the cake on the selected serving dish and slip pieces of wax paper under the edges of the cake. After you have iced or frosted the cake, gently slide out the wax paper. This process will prevent you from making a mess of your serving plate.

Leeks, cleaning

Remove the hairs at the root of the leek, leaving the core behind. Slice the leek the long way through the greens to the stem in four pieces. Rinse well under cold water. Leeks keep a lot of their grit, so wash them thoroughly.

Lemon juice

Always refers to freshly squeezed juice. Remove the pits, but do try to keep the pulp—it adds flavor.

Milk substitutes

For 1 cup (250 mL) whole milk, you can substitute as follows:

$2/3$ cup (150 mL) 1% plus $1/3$ cup (100 mL) half-and-half

OR

$3/4$ cup (175 mL) 2% plus $1/4$ cup (50 mL) half-and-half

For buttermilk, see page 263.

Oil, cooking with

Whenever I cook with oil (not butter), I preheat the sauté pan, then heat the oil, and then add the ingredients.

Olive oil

Always use extra-virgin. I save the good stuff for salads and use a less expensive brand for cooking.

Pasta or vegetables, cooking

Always add enough kosher or coarse salt to pasta or vegetable cooking water so that it tastes like the sea.

If you want to keep the color of green vegetables, boil them in a very large amount of water, cook them rapidly, and then shock them in ice water to seize the color.

If you want perfectly cooked pasta, boil it in a very large amount of water.

Peaches, peeling

Cut an "X" in the blossom ends of the washed peaches. Blanch them in a saucepan of boiling water for 15 seconds. Remove with a slotted spoon and transfer them to ice water to stop the cooking. The skin will now peel off the peaches easily.

Peppers, roasting and peeling

Preheat the oven to broil. Place sweet peppers (works with any color) on a cookie sheet lined with foil. Turn the peppers often with tongs, and cook them until they're browned on all sides. Watch them carefully, as they tend to cook quickly and can get away from you. Cool the peppers in a paper bag, then remove the skin by rubbing it off with a paper towel or your fingers. Try not to wash the peppers or you'll remove all the great juice the roasting created.

Pie Crusts

Keep the following 10 steps in mind when preparing a pie crust:

1. The butter and/or shortening should be frozen.

2. The water should be iced.

3. The flour should be put in the freezer for about 10 minutes or in the bowl of a food processor in the refrigerator for about 20 minutes to ensure that all the ingredients are really cold.

4. Do not overwork the dough, either in mixing or in rolling it out, in order to keep the frozen pieces of butter and shortening firm. This is what makes the pie crust flaky.

5. When adding water, keep in mind that you will require less on warm summer days.

6. Let the dough rest for at least 1 hour in the refrigerator. When you take it out, you can let it stand for about 5 minutes to remove the chill for ease of rolling.

7. Lightly flour the board or marble and roll from the center of the dough to the outside edge, moving the dough to ensure that it doesn't stick.

8. Turn the pie plate upside down over the dough, cut a circle 2" (5 cm) larger than the pie plate, and beautifully crimp the edge of the crust.

9. A 9" (23 cm) pie plate holds about 4 cups (1 L) of filling and serves 8.

10. I bake my pies, especially the fruit ones, on a pastry saver or a baking sheet that has been lined with a silpat pad or parchment paper. Keeps the oven cleaner! I also wrap the edges of the crust with foil so that they don't brown too much.

Poultry skin

I try to never pierce the skin of the poultry or the flesh of the meat I'm cooking. I'm convinced that toughens the texture.

Saucing pasta

When saucing pasta, I always add 1 tablespoon (15 mL) butter for extra richness as a final touch. After draining the cooked pasta, I reserve at least 1 cup (250 mL) of the pasta water in case I need to thin a sauce.

To thicken your sauce, add an uncooked, unpeeled potato to the sauce for the last 15 minutes. Don't forget to remove the potato!

Shrimp, cleaning

You will be able to remove the shell by pulling the tendrils from the inside of the shrimp. I like to leave the tail on for presentation. With the tip of a sharp paring knife, cut into the back of the shrimp and pull out the black vein. Rinse and pat dry.

Tomatoes, peeling

Cut an "X" in the bottom of the washed tomatoes and submerge them in boiling water for a moment or two. Check the bottoms to see if the tomatoes will peel easily. Remove them from the water, being careful to take them out before they cook! Peel, core, and coarsely chop the tomatoes.

Vanilla sugar

Remove the seeds from a vanilla pod and mix the seeds and the pods into 1 cup (250 mL) sugar. It's a good idea to always have some vanilla sugar prepared to use for baking and even for coffee. Great taste. Vanilla sugar will keep stored in the pantry for months in a covered container.

Index

Entries set in *italics* indicate tips